DR JOHNSON'S DICTIONARY OF MODERN LIFE

DR JOHNSON'S DICTIONARY OF MODERN LIFE

Tom Morton

FOR SQUARE PEG PUBLISHERS,

AN IMPRINT OF RANDOM HOUSE

Published by Square Peg 2010
2 4 6 8 10 9 7 5 3

First published in Great Britain in 2010 by Square Peg
Random House, 20 Vauxhall Bridge Road, London SW1V 2SA

www.rbooks.co.uk

Addresses for companies within
The Random House Group Limited can be found at:
www.randomhouse.co.uk/offices.htm

The Random House Group Limited Reg. No. 954009

A CIP catalogue record for this book
is available from the British Library

ISBN 9780224086684

The Random House Group Limited supports
The Forest Stewardship Council (FSC), the leading international forest certification
organisation. All our titles that are printed on Greenpeace approved
FSC certified paper carry the FSC logo. Our paper procurement
policy can be found at www.rbooks.co.uk/environment

Mixed Sources
Product group from well-managed
forests and other controlled sources
www.fsc.org   Cert no. TT-COC-2139
© 1996 Forest Stewardship Council
FSC

Typeset by Palimpsest Book Production Ltd, Falkirk, Stirlingshire
Printed in Great Britain by Clays Ltd, St Ives plc

FOREWORD

To everything a name, it is said. Or at least, it sounds like something that is said. Perhaps it is not said. Perhaps I misheard. Nonetheless, it sounds like good advice. Without words, these things we call 'things' would remain anonymous, mysterious, even dangerous. 'Look out, there's a long whatsit with a sort of . . . pointed mouth and no legs . . . and it's . . .'

Too late. Your companion is dead.

Earlier reference works performed this function well enough. Doctor Johnson's first dictionary recently helped me discover that the thing living in my upstairs toilet was not, as I feared, a rat, but a small, dirty fox. With its tremendous page-count, I was also able to use the dictionary to make short work of both fox and toilet.

An invaluable reference work, then. So why do I recommend that you place this volume right alongside it?

Because it seems to me that Doctor Johnson and his online Amanuenses have between them created an analogue version of the guide that gave *The Hitchhiker's Guide To The Galaxy* its title. Unlike Douglas Adam's creation, a magical travel book that covers life, the universe and everything, the good Doctor's book only covers our immediate surroundings, but each entry is written with such acuity that those surroundings are suddenly transformed, and we, dumbstruck Arthur Dents, see them anew.

Gritting ✈ *ger.*
Winter Activity of which Mention is never made, except by Reference to its not having taken PLACE

Pete DOHERTY ✈ *n.*
callow Waif who does battle 'gainst the twin Forces of Opium & the Magistrate with merely a Lute & a Poetry-Book

Snakes On A Plane ✈ *n.*
a drama prais'd for the Directness of its TITLE; then damn'd by the Directness of its REVIEWS

Booker Prize ✈ *n.*
Cabal of Necromancers & Shamen meeting once yearly to endow but one Book with mythick Popularity

An analogue pleasure that had a digital birth. Without the Internet, The Good Doctor would never have benefitted from the creative possibilities of a Twitter account. And, if confronted alone, an enterprise such as this might flounder. But The Doctor had plenty of help because Twitter brought him into contact with the Amanuenses and Patrons mentioned at the end of this book. (I go by @Glinner on Twitter, and I take great pride in my role in persuading Doctor Johnson to commit these definitions to paper.)

This book is, in fact, one of those everyday miracles of the information age that have become so common-place we never recognise them as such. But miracle it

is, because Samuel Johnson, in the form of those qualities he embodied, lives again within the pages of this
book.

Graham Linehan
2010

INTRODUCTION

It is the Fate of those who toil at the lower Employments of Life, to be rather driven by the Fear of Evil, than attracted by the Prospect of Good; to be expos'd to Censure, without Hope of Praise; to be disgrac'd by Miscarriage, or punish'd for Neglect, where Success would have been without **APPLAUSE** & Diligence without **REWARD**.

Among these unhappy Mortals is the Writer of **DICTIONARIES**; whom Mankind have consider'd the Pioneer of Literature, doom'd only to remove Rubbish & clear Obstructions from the Paths through which Learning and Genius press forward to Conquest & Glory, without bestowing a Smile on the humble **DRUDGE** that facilitates their Progress.

My earlier Dictionary did receive some little Acclaim, yet it struggl'd for Relevance; for the World it sought to parse & define had mov'd **ONWARD**. In the Manner of an untended Garden, I did turn my Back for what seem'd like an Instant; only to observe it wither'd by the Asides of Mister Simon **COWELL**, festoon'd with vulgar **BILL-BOARDS** & o'ergrown with the present-tense Peacockery of the **FACE-BOOK**.

For no Plant or Vine does grow as heartily, nor merit pruning as ardently as human **FOLLY**.

Modern Life does come in nigh-on infinite Varieties. Thus Men replete with more Options than Sense shall likely hasten down Paths of Error shod in Mister **UGG'S** ovine Boots or brandishing Mister **NINTENDO's** Japann'd Idiot-Wand.

And Merchants shall happily indulge the Deficiencies & Whims of the dunce-like Publick; unto the Extent of forewarning of the lurking Presence of **NUTS** in a Sack of Nuts, or provisioning a Coffee-House with such great Hogsheads of sweeten'd, froth'd Milk to adumbrate a once-fine Cup of bitter Stimulant into a Weaning-Brew for a mere **INFANT.** Commercial Novelty awaits round every Corner, as surely as Cut-Purses might await in every darken'd Alley.

Then the popular Press-Men, the electronick Post & the hysterick Town-Criers of four-and-twenty Hour Television do combine to spread News of any such Folly hither & yon amongst the Populace as surely as a Rat does spread the Ague or a Frenchman does spread the **POX.**

My Duty as a Humble Lexicographer is once again to clear the path, forsaking Spade & Scythe for Mister **JOBS'** venerat'd Tablet. I would strive to impose some basick Categorisation 'pon the Mores & the Personalities that do Characterise modern Life. The Pomposity of Mister **WINNER,** the vitreous Computing of Mister Wm. **GATES,** e'en the popp'd Cocoa of Mister **KELLOGG:** all shall find themselves rightly defin'd & lampoon'd herein.

Shorn of the motley Band of Amanuenses who labour'd 'pon my Dictionary of 1755, I have found many Volunteers thro' the electronick Means of **TWITTER,** a Tavern of the Æther, where congregate Men shy of Work but generous of Verbiage, so much so that they do cap their Contributions at seven Score Characters. Some Definitions have appear'd already in that most fleeting Medium; most Definitions & relat'd Commentary herein have been compos'd for this very Volume.

The very Commitment of a contemporary Topick unto Paper does bring with it inherent Peril, for the Labour of a modern Lexicographer is less Herculean than Sisyphean & the constant Eruption of popular Oafishness might easily o'erwhelm a once-definitive Compendium. My greatest Fear, save for the Debtors' Hulk or the **Gout**, is that a breeding Pair of Miss Peppa **Pig** & Mister Postman **Pat** shall sire further Swathes of the **BALDERDASH** of modern Life as yet to be captur'd in my Dictionary. I shall thus let any further Novelties find their own low way in the World.

In all such Dictionaries, the Fault of any egregious Mis-definition is purely my own.

Yet the **FOLLIES**, dear Readers, do belong to us **ALL**.

A *is for* ARCADE

ABBA ⇸ *n.*
four Quarterns of Vikings most obvious in Rhyming
Couplets; yet most mysterious as to who is the **FIT ONE**

Acid House ⇸ *n.*
repetitive Charivari typical of the far Principalities
of Detroit & **IBIZA**; much improv'd by Æther &
LAUDANUM

Adam and the Ants ⇸ *n.*
vile Band of Dandies & Highway-men who thus deserve
naught save the Scaffold & the **GIBBET**

Aga ⇸ *n.*
iron-clad theologickal Device to prepare a pompous
Person for Hell by contriving a Furnace in his Kitchen

Airport Lounge ⇸ *n.*
parody of a Sitting-Room or Mme **POMPADOUR**'s
Salon; oft a Hive for Dullards clad in Mister **LEVI**'s
Docker Pantaloons

A Level ⇸ *n.*
qualifickation proving a Youth's Intelleckt & Standing;
three do earn Entrie to the fine University of **KEELE**

Alton Towers ⇸ *n.*
purgatory in Staffordshire: Man is condemn'd to stand
in Line with his grimmest Fellows awaiting Fates of
Food or Propulsion

Ambridge ⇸ *n.*
imaginary Village: diſputes over its suppos'd Nature &
Status do make it a Rival unto **GOD**'s own Heaven

Angels ⇸ *n.*
mawkish Dirge of grinning Cadaver Maſter Robbie
WILLIAMS, oft heard at a maudlin Carouse or the
Obsequies of a Peasant-Child

Arcade ⇸ *n.*
Palace of Diversions, home to a Table of Hockey upon
the Air, Dance Dance **REVOLUTION** & Queſt with the
ruby Light call'd **LAZER**

Atkins Diet ⇸ *n.*
patent Regimen for reducing Corpulence by dining
solely on **MEAT**; a Diet endors'd by famously willow-like
Monarch Henry VIII

A Is For Advertising

Advertising is oft defin'd as the moſt base of the commercial Arts, whereby Representation is parted from Truth
in the Service of **PEDLARS & MERCHANTMEN.**

A Woman may be compell'd to partake in the moſt
extreme of Sports while confin'd by Menſtruation,
should she follow the Counsel of the Advertiser, argue
its Criticks. A Man should believe that all future

Journeys shall be taken on the deserted Hill-Roads of Tuscany, should Carriage-Purchase be true to that depicted in Advertisements.

Many Advertisers do attempt to berate the Publick in to a Purchase. Thus Cillit Bang is a wondrous Elixir for the Purpose of keeping Farthings & Pennies clean of the Filth of the Mob, according to the Admonitions of Mister Barry SCOTT. And Ronseal is proclaim'd Prince of Varnishes, on account of its tin-said Efficacy. The Market-Town of Halifax has enslav'd its poor Citizenry to act as Mummers for its great BANK.

It is oft suppos'd that the Publick are dumb as Cows, most easily led & entreat'd to part with scarce SPECIE in Exchange for well-promoted Trifles.

Yet any Observer of the Publick would know that the Englishman will expend above his true Income & Needs at the merest Provockation: from the simple Temptation of a Jar of Embrocation with five-and-twenty per cent FREE, unto the merry Delusion that a Man may become the most rakish Gadabout should he purchase Meinherr Ferdinand PORSCHE'S Swabian Sporting-Carriage. To attribute this human Folly unto Advertising is to mistake a jolly Accompaniment for an actual Cause: it is as if to blame the Juniper-Berry for the Ills of Gin-Drinking, or the Guardsman's Bearskin for the Waging of War.

Withal the watching Publick does permit the Pedlar great Leeway in the Depiction of his WARES, should he be entertaining about it. Thus the English do expect all such Messages to be accompany'd peradventure by a Monster that seeks Honey, an Iron-clad Visitant from a neighbouring Planet that extols the Mashing of Potatoes, a Monkey that does Drum, or the Unleashing of a Cavalcade of colour'd Balls.

Herewith defin'd the Works & Wiles of Advertising:

Advertising Agency ↦ *n.*
part bawdy Tavern & learned High-Table, artfully guis'd as an Enterprise of Business

Banner ↦ *n.*
worthless electronick Handbill that gulls the Reader to believe that he is the one-millionth of his Kind

Celebrity Endorsement ↦ *n.*
Act of Transubstantiation that does sanctify Shaving Cutlasses & Hair-Balms by the Touch of prominent Personages

Creatives ↦ *n.*
motley Cabal of Cut-Purses, Lollygaggers, Mollys & Fops, each clutching Folios fill'd with Promise yet devoid of Idea

Jingle ↦ *n.*
cant Doggerel beseeching the Masses to go forth & compare or commit the conjoin'd Acts of Shaking & VAC-ING

Logo ⇸ *n.*
Medallion, rightly us'd as a Mark of Excellence &
Provenance, more oft us'd to bedeck the Clothing of
Ruffians & Nincompoops

Mascot ⇸ *n.*
dumb Animal press'd in to Service to hawk a Merchant's
Wares, thus a Tiger may promote frosted Rice or
Carriage-Oil

Slogan ⇸ *n.*
summary of Wares, mark'd by Shortage of Words &
Paucity of Grammar, viz. Think Different; The Future Is
Orange

A Is For America

The American Colonies are the most fascinating Lands for
those who wish to observe the human Condition, yet the
most perplexing for the harmless Drudge who wishes to
define it. 'Tis not enough to speak as Mrs Judith
CHALMERS and thoughtlessly call America a Land of
Contrast, for in truth it is a Land of flat-out Contradiction,
all of which does confound any simple Definition.

Observ'd: 'tis both a Land of the most upstanding
States-men, from Mister Benj. **FRANKLIN** to President
Josiah **BARTLET** & to the lowliest Rogues, such as Messrs
Geo. **BUSH**, Avon **BARKSDALE** & Michael **MOUSE**.

'Tis a Land where the common Felon may be gass'd by Poison, shot by Fusillade, or roasted by Mister FARADAY'S Electricity; yet also where the most artful Rendering of the Land is in the movable Etchings of Criminality call'd Grand Theft AUTO.

'Tis a Land that had hop'd to purge the grim Bile of Slavery by eleckting Mister OBAMA unto the high Office of President, yet does now intrigue & conspire to make the Presidency into the worst Job in America.

'Tis a Land where Form & Custom are oft invert'd: a Glass of Claret with Luncheon in New Amsterdam is as scandalous as a Tincture of Opium in London.

America is Home both to Millions of Citizens who endeavour to perfeckt the human Form and to yet further Millions whose great ARSES can only be contain'd by Acres of Broad-Cloth engineer'd in to CHINOS.

As a new Republick, America is prone to the twin Follies of Optimism & Novelty. The Man who invents the Sandwich of broil'd Beef can aspire to the highest Status in the Land; whilst the Man who gives said Beef-Sandwich a jocular Name & places a Slice of Cheese athwart it is hail'd as the greatest Inventor of the AGE. All of which is great Sport unto the Englishman, who does know full well that Life is liv'd in Humour & characteris'd by DISAPPOINTMENT.

As grave as the Insult of crying Independence from His MAJESTY King Geo. III, the American Colonists do grievous Injurie unto the English Language. 'Tis most confounding: apparently to have one's Ass serv'd on a Plate is not an exotick Dinner, but to lose Esteem in an **ARGUMENT**. Likewise, American **YOUTHS** oft employ 'Do You Know What I Am Saying?' as a Suffix in Speech. To which I reply, 'Yes, **BARELY**.'

Fortunately a boundless Land inhabit'd by vexatious Enthusiasts does give Rise to endless note-worthy Curiosities:

Cadillac ⇸ *n.*
vulgar Chariot, much desir'd by Americans. It does look like a Cow in black **ARMOUR**

The American, in canting Tribute unto the Environment, enacts Laws that no Carriage should consume more Coal + Coke than every single Forge + Foundry in all **SHEFFIELD**

Frosting; Home-Fries ⇸ *n.*
cant Terms that enable the American to smuggle great Hogsheads of **FAT** in to his Diet

Midwest ⇸ *n.*
blasted Tundra 'twixt Coasts, where the Populace is fed by Corn & cloth'd by **CATALOGUE**

Oatmeal ⇸ *n.*
in England, a Grain fed to Horses; in New Amsterdam Hotels, a twenty-eight-Dollar **BREAKFAST**

Superbowl ⤳ *n.*
Phenomenon that is like a Sea-Monster unto an Englishman's Mind: from far Oceans, most dramatick, fearsome & **INCOMPREHENSIBLE**

Thanksgiving ⤳ *n.*
American festival mark'd by the twin Abominations of marshmallow'd Sweet-Potato & slain **INDIAN**

B

B *is for* BURGER KING

Bad → *adj.*
i. possess'd of the Quality of Badness; ii. **GOOD**

> *The Adjective Bad-Ass'd is of the same Derivation; it bears*
> *no Relation unto the troubling Humours of the Back-Body*
> *when one undertakes a Four-Week Voyage unto the*
> *Colonies with scant Provisions save Weevil-Biscuit &*
> *Porto-Wine*

Barbecue → *n.*
Englishman's Summer Repast, compos'd in equal Parts
of cann'd Ale, Charcoal & **RAIN-WATER**

BBC 3 → *n.*
an electronick Theatre aim'd at an ingrate Audience of
bawdy Apprentices & Orphan-Lads

> *The very Charter of BBC 3 does compel the electronick*
> *Theatre to offer Employment unto dough-pudgy Idiot-Boy*
> *Master James* **CORDEN** *& to proffer the short Commons*
> *of two Pints of lagered* **ALE** *& a Burlap of* **CRISPS**. *'Tis*
> *thought that BBC 3 draws its Power from a great*
> **DYNAMO** *of my Lord* **REITH** *spinning in his* **GRAVE**

Bling → *n., adj.*
gaudy Filigree of Silver & Gold Plate, that does gild
otherwise unremarkable Voids of Character

Blog → *n.*
electronick Diary unto which earnest Fools do commit their innermost Thoughts, safe that no Man shall ever read them

James BOND → *n.*
lowly Scotch Footpad in a Dandy's Weskit, sent abroad to LIE for his Country

BOOTS → *n.*
grim Apotheckary at which a white-rob'd Shill of a Woman may proffer a Tub of Monsieur L'OREAL'S patent Cream

Botox → *n.*
merely the Pox inject'd into the Brow by a Barber-Surgeon; a capital INVENTION

Brazilian → *adj.*
to be shorn athwart the Nethers & Privy-Piece, a common Agony of the Fashionable

Britain's Got Talent → *n.*
questionable Assertion; yet Britain does possess OAFS, BUFFOONS & a cretinous Voting-Publick

Budweiser → *n.*
Messrs ANHEUSER & BUSCH take the Prussian Art of Brewing & adulterate it to bring forth yellowish WATER

Burger KING ⇸ *n.*
majeſtic Monarch of broil'd Meats, like fellow King
WENCESLAS, he does Succour the hardscrabble
Peasantry

B Is For Books

It would be moſt negligent of a Lexicographer to with-
hold Comment 'pon the notable Practitioners of Words.
For each Year, thousands of Tomes do ſpring forth, shel-
tering like Saplings 'neath the mighty Oaks of pubescent
Thaumaturge Maſter Harry **POTTER** & bellicose
Colonial Miſter Thomas **CLANCY**, each bearing further
Renderings of the English Language. To underſtand
Books is to underſtand the Crafting of English, the
Concerns of the letter'd Publick & e'en to fathom the
relentless Assault 'pon good Sense of Miſter Dan
BROWN.

Enumerat'd hereunder the beſt-selling Definitions &
Aphorisms:

Angela's Ashes ⇸ *n.*
Childhood Account of Damnation, Dole & Typhoid;
hence it remains the moſt agreeable Depiction of Life in
Hibernia

Booker Prize ⇢ *n.*
Cabal of Necromancers & Shamen meeting once yearly
to endow but one Book with mythick Popularity

Bravo Two Zero ⇢ *n.*
shadow-dwelling Red-coat Mister Andrew **McNab's**
Mesopotamian Farce of Musketry, mislaid Carriages &
wily Goat-Herds

Chick Lit ⇢ *adj.* Fiction of Slatterns accurs'd with two
Lodgings, three Paid Employments, four Consorts &
one ardent Intent to have it all

Cookery Book ⇢ *n.*
once a Volume of Instruction for the Housewife, now an
Author's Diatribe 'pon their idyllick Life interwov'n
with **Cake**

The Da Vinci Code ⇢ *n.*
Conspiracy Screed: uncertain whether the greater
Conspirator is Opus Dei or Mister **Brown** 'gainst the
reading Publick

Fever Pitch ⇢ *n.*
Mister **Hornby**, incapable of expressing Sentiment save
thro' Sports-Men, thus endears himself to Others of
equal Inability

Ghost Writer ⇢ *n.*
hidden Drudge, frequently compell'd to fashion the verbal
Clay of Mistress Katie **Price** into Clods of near Sense

Gina FORD ⇥ *n.*
harsh Governess whose Screeds 'pon the Rearing of
Infants do preserve the moſt admirable Cuſtoms of
Centuries paſt

For Dummies ⇥ *n.*
series of Treatises that may inſtruckt the Reader in all
worldly Matters save how not to patronise with a Book-
Title

The God Delusion ⇥ *n.*
Whereby, white-hair'd Patriarch **DAWKINS** brings forth
a weighty Tome of Morals to inveigh 'gainſt the same
from **GOD**

Harry Potter ⇥ *n.*
Wizard whose greateſt Spells have made Publick
Schools acceptable to the Masses and Infant-Books
acceptable unto Adults

Men Are From Mars ⇥ *n.*
cant colonial Parsing of wherefore the Sexes do differ:
less to benefit the Wise than to give Fodder unto the
Stand-up Comick

Miſter Men ⇥ *n.*
Geometrickals whose Parents had the Prescience to
name them after their defining Characteriſtick:
CLEVER, BUMP, TICKLE, &c

Oprah's Book Club ⇸ *n.*
sacrificial Altar 'pon which deſperate Authors warm
human Hearts to placate th'omnipotent Miss WINFREY

That's Not My . . . ⇸ *n.*
a Bhagavad Gita for suckling Infants in which a few
tactile Fabricks do ſtand for an infinity of Subjeckt
Matters

C *is for* CONCRETE

Cage Fighting ⇸ *n.*
fearsome Confinement of the Laws of the Jungle & the
Rules of QUEENSBERRY into an iron Bear-Pit

Car Boot Sale ⇸ *n.*
Parade of brok'n CHATTELS sold to purchase further
Trash, ſtrong ALE and Dutch JENNIVER; thus the Circle
e'er turns

Cassette ⇸ *n.*
Case of ſpindle-mounted Ribbons, carefully concealing
the cultural Legacy of the nineteen eighties

Cavolo Nero ⇸ *n.*
humble Cabbage that inveigles its Way into fashionable
Company thro' its Italianate Name; a DANCING-
MASTER of Vegetables

Chattering Classes ⇸ *n.*
polite Opinion, veſt'd with mythickal Power, as if
Gentlefolk ſteer'd the Ship of State 'twixt Slices of
Carrot-Cake

Children In Need ⇸ *n.*
mawkish Revel for Infants in Want of CARE & Adults in
Want of ATTENTION:

> *'Sir, pray ſponsor ten* GUINEAS *for my Endeavour to sit in
> a Bathing-Tub fill'd with* FRENCHMEN *& Porto* WINE,
> *'tis for Children in Need'*

Cider ⇝ *n.*
APPLE-JACK belov'd by Scallywags for its Potency, by Miniſters as a Source of Excise & by **WURZELS** as it befits their **BRAND**

Cigarette ⇝ *n.*
a fine Method both to flavour the **LUNGS** & to support the Commerce of the Virginia Rebels

Coalition ⇝ *n.*
Combine that places all politickal Parties at the Helm; thus the moſt fear'd Form of Government

Coldplay ⇝ *n.*
Puritan Seĉt forbidd'n from allowing any Joy from their great Wealth, comely Wives & popular Acclaim to seep into their **MUSICK**

Compaĉt Disc ⇝ *n.*
mirror'd Medallion, firſt smelt'd as a Conduit into the World for the Works of **DIRE STRAITS** & thus a Tool for Diaboliſts

Comparison Site ⇝ *n.*
eleĉtrick Market-Place where Swathes of Insurance-Agents, Scalpers & Middle-Men bid for yr. Cuſtom; an unsightly Jouſt

Conference-Call ⇝ *n.*
Mechanickal Impossibility wherein a Fool attempts to be closer to his Fellows by shouting in to a **BARREL**

Cool Britannia ⇢ *n.*
short-liv'd Epoch mark'd by transient Pop-Minstrels, so
nam'd for it induces Shivers in those who recall it

> *Most egregious Signs of the Cool Britannia Era: ginger-
> tressed Harpy Miss Geraldine* HALLIWELL, *clad in a
> Frock of th'Union Flag, believ'd herself to be the*
> BOUDICCA *of the Age; Lute-Troll Mister Noel*
> GALLAGHER *invit'd unto Downing Street as an Affront
> both to his Dignity & to that of the Prime Minister*

Concrete ⇢ *n.*
dun greyish Admixture, from which may be fashioned
Ramps, Balustrades, Sewers & the City of
BIRMINGHAM

Conference-Centre ⇢ *n.*
Destruction of a grand Country-Mansion, where boil'd
MINTS & Decanters fill'd with LIME CORDIAL pass for
Hospitality

Congestion Charge ⇢ *n.*
Excise that does pick the Pocket of him who DRIVES in
London as surely as the Cut-Purse does to him who
WALKS in London

Conservative ⇢ *adj.*
 in Politicks, inclin'd to preserve Tradition; in political
Parties, inclin'd to preserve Wealth

Council Tax ↣ *n.*
Levy 'pon the Home to fund domeſtick Services &
according to fever'd Conſpirators, to fund secret Cabals
of **Bin-Spies**

Creationism ↣ *n.*
scientifick Cant where Fossils are said to teſt the
Faithful & Claims are made to teſt the **Patience**

Crocs ↣ *n.*
Idiot-Badge for the **Feet**

Cuſtoms ↣ *n.*
of a Country, its formal Manners & Courtesy; in an Airport, their **Absence**

C Is For Celebrity

To the time-honour'd Ranks of Society – Monarchy,
Ariſtockracy, Nobility, Yeomanry, middle-Management,
Peasantry, Welch-Men – a new Rank is add'd: that of
Celebrity.

To-day, a man can scarcely pick up a Penny-Handbill
or empty his Chamber-Pot without encountering that
populous Creature call'd **Celebrity**. An humble
Barber, a sauce-ſplash'd Cook, a retir'd Town-Crier or
e'en an ambitious **Harlot** who does ensnare a Sports-
man: all have the Status of **Celebrity** beſtow'd 'pon

them. Indeed, the lowlieſt Man who unblocks the Privy, if bless'd with Ivory Dentition & an eveningtide Assignation with a Strumpet, would today be hail'd as a Celebrity Night-soilman.

Those with the Status of Celebrity, much like a Freeman of a City, do exercise divers Privileges, to wit: endorsing Foodſtuffs; promoting SCENTS with their very Name; holding Court 'pon the great Issues of the Day, as if a televis'd Almanack of the Year should be legitimis'd by their vapid Opinions & being the Subjeckt of sordid Etchings depickting their Loss & Gain of WEIGHT.

The poor Celebrity does make a damnable Paċt whereby his Status is gain'd by trading every laſt Farthing of his Privacy. Now the Publick does demand to see these wretched Creatures at home & at Reſt, as if it were an Englishman's RIGHT to eſpy the Wedding-Etchings, Tavern Frolicks & dream new Home of any Person deem'd Celebrity.

Like a Farmer who does find his Crops devour'd by Locuſts, or a Landowner who does find his Garden o'er-run with Tinkers, one might rightly ask whence came these CELEBRITIES? 'Tis a Matter, as my friend Miſter Adam SMITH would remark, of SUPPLY & DEMAND: today's endless SUPPLY of News-Print & minor Channels 'pon the Idiot-Lantern does DEMAND an equally endless Volume of Tittle-Tattle to occupy its Space. Thus vapid Charaċters of low Birth & cunning do come to beſtride the great Stage of CELEBRITY. It is a Status conferr'd not by Virtue or Abilitie or noble Birth but by the publick GAZE.

For Readers who lack the Time to envisit Bedlam or the Stomach to peruse the Chap-Book call'd *Hello!* herewith some Celebrities 'pon which to GAZE:

Messrs ANT & DEC ⇢ *n.pl.*
Duet of Northumbrian Boy-Jesters whose great Fame and great For'heads do expand e'er WIDER

Kevin BACON ⇢ *n.*
footloose Thespian of limited Ability; inexplicably the NEXUS 'pon which the entire World of DRAMA does turn

Victoria BECKHAM ⇢ *n.*
Ghost at the Feast of Fashion & popular Musick, seemingly constructed from a Skeleton & two Oranges

Adrian CHILES ⇢ *n.*
jovial meat-fac'd Foetus, entitl'd to speak for the Nation for he is the Better of NO ONE

Jeremy CLARKSON ⇢ *n.*
curl-crown'd King Midas for a stupid Age; everything 'pon which he pronounces does become Night-Soil.

Characteristick pronouncements from Mister **CLARKSON'S** *Bully-Pulpit might include: 'I favour Sausages,* **PHAETONS & CARRIAGES**. *I abhor*

*Frenchmen & **SODOMY**,' and 'I cannot be a **DANDY**, for I ride Mister **HUMMER**'s weighty Coach'*

Alice COOPER ↣ *n.*
Once fearsome Performer who now draws a Pension and ekes out his Twilight years in divers Comedies & **ADVERTISEMENTS**

*Mister Igworth **POP** is of that same ilk*

Peter CROUCH ↣ *n.*
Sporting Gilly-Gaupus; an athletick Man imprison'd in the Body of a great **CRANE-FLY**

Pete DOHERTY ↣ *n.*
callow Waif who does battle 'gainst the twin Forces of Opium & the Magistrate with merely a Lute & a Poetry-Book

*Master **DOHERTY** does leave a Trail of Damage in his Wake, from Women enslav'd unto Laudanum to whimsy-blight'd Lyricks*

Danny DYER ↣ *n.*
cockney Actor, oft us'd as a Cypher for the entire Criminal & Cudgel-Wielding Classes of England

*Master **DYER** does affeckt a Cockney Dialeckt said to be Imperceptible to all save Messrs **CHAS & DAVE**. E'en the most coarse Tilbury Dock-Labourer would be unable to apprehend the Meaning behind Master **DYER'S*** *embolden'd Doggerel of 'Pwoper Naughty' & 'Mugg'd Off'*

Bryan FERRY ↝ *n.*
Son of a Durham Collier, once embolden'd to dress as a Dandy, who now carries himself as a **DUKE**

Stephen FRY ↝ *n.*
effete moral Light-House: his very Name carries a Mark of Wisdom & his Views do guide the moral Sentiment of the genteel **MOB**

Noel GALLAGHER ↝ *n.*
pugilistick Caveman who left his Oasis Troupe after sixteen Years & one Melody

> *Mister **GALLAGHER** & his simian Brother are quite the Punch and Judy of our Age. The Publick do flock to see them Brawl 'pon Stage: on rare Occasion a Song will break out. Mister **GALLAGHER** is of some Reknown 'pon the Lute, for he can bring forth fewer than six Notes from its six Strings*

Paul GASCOIGNE ↝ *n.*
Agglomeration of base human Tics & Impulses, barely contain'd in a mess of Bleach & Sinew

Rolf HARRIS ↝ *n.*
aspirating transported Convict of such uncertain artistick Talent that he oft asks the Publick to guess what he has limn'd

Jools HOLLAND ↣ *n.*
Unctuous Cockney-Oik who does earn the Trust of Musickians & then does assault them with his **FORTE-PIANO**

Michael JACKSON ↣ *n.*
deceas'd freaklike Albino, remember'd for his ghoulish **DANCE** & misplac'd **LOVE** for Monkeys & **INFANTS**

> *Fool* **JACKSON**, *as all forlorn Prophets, does draw a motley Band of Idolators, each of whom attempts to perform a fiendish moral Calculus whereby the Status of proficient Dancer does cancel the Status of proficient Pederast. Learn'd Magistrates should be wary of any Defendant who does plead Innocence on Account of wearing a sequin-bedeck'd Glove & performing an elaborate 'Walk-'pon-the-Moon'*

Boris JOHNSON ↣ *n.*
High Tory Scare-Crow; at Time of Writing Mayor; at Time of Publishing a Minister, sham'd Jester or haul'd to the Gallows

Lorraine KELLY ↣ *n.*
lachrymose Town-Crier who gives **SUCCOUR** unto the **INDOLENT** & drives godly Men unto their Work

Paul McCARTNEY ↣ *n.*
aloft-thumb'd Lute-Player, more belov'd for his Choice of Melodies than for his Choice of **WIVES**

Malcolm McLAREN ⇸ *n.*
lament'd Fairground Barker, promoter of Sex Musketry
& Hemped-Rope Skipping in the Dutch Manner

George MICHAEL ⇸ *n.*
sedated Hellenic Troubadour who by Night does
affright the Denizens of Hampstead Heath &
unsuspecting Coachmen

> *Those who would seek to understand the Ways of the Molly
> should make close Study of Messrs* **MICHAEL &
> RIDGELEY'S** *lusty fancy-dress'd Grand Tour so docu-
> ment'd as Club Tropicana*

Dannii MINOGUE ⇸ *n.*
waxen Shrew support'd by twin pillars of sibling Fame
& frozen Features

Piers MORGAN ⇸ *n.*
boorish Newspaperman; in Appearance the Love-Child
of Messrs David **CAMERON** & Richard **GERVAIS**

Nick RHODES ⇸ *n.*
flaxen-hair'd once-pretty Wench, paint'd with Rouge &
Mercury-Cake

Keith RICHARDS ⇸ *n.*
wither'd Minstrel whose now-frail Body is compos'd
entirely of Skin-Folds, Opium & Pirate-Tales

Wayne ROONEY ↠ *n.*
bruising Lancastrian Sports-Oaf, whose Face was carv'd
by almighty **GOD** from a **POTATO**

J.K. ROWLING ↠ *n.*
authoress fam'd for two Acts of Diabolism: writing of
Witch-Craft & amassing a Fortune then choosing to
dwell in **SCOTLAND**

Sir Jimmy SAVILE ↠ *n.*
senescent Harlequin, whose Cigars, betinted Eye-
Glasses & yodell'd Tongue should rightly repel Infants
but do not

> *He who dares attempt to document the Life of* **SAVILE** *for
> an unfamiliar Publick must first prove that he is not a
> fictional Creation, a Grotesque dream'd by Messrs
> Timothy* **BURTON** *or Terence* **GILLIAM** *as a cautionary
> Tale for Infants or for those who do commission Series of
> Entertainment for the Magick-Lantern.* **SAVILE**, *tho' in his
> ninth Decade, does run to Distance as did Phidippides
> himself. He does dress as gaudily as colonial Troubadours*
> **RUN DMC**, *bedeck'd with sufficient Medallions as to
> attract a Raiding-Party of Corsairs. He presents himself as
> a* **MEPHISTOPHELES** *unto England's Youth, promising to
> indulge their wildest Ambitions of which yr. Letters are but
> only the Start*

Herr Michael SCHUMACHER ⇸ *n.*
quicksilver Prussian Coachman, fuell'd by Tallow-Oil &
Hubris

Jon SNOW ⇸ *n.*
lanky Town-Crier fam'd for his Jacobin Views & jaunty
Cravats

Rod STEWART ⇸ *n.*
salt-preserv'd Troubadour whose great Range has
enabl'd him to be Scottish, black, married, faithful &
e'en **YOUNG**

Michael WINNER ⇸ *n.*
corpulent Man-Cushion much giv'n to issuing forth
Procklamations 'pon Foodstuffs & 'pon his own great
Status

C Is For Christmas

A most fertile Subjeckt, the Festival of Christmas does
combine Traditions both Pagan & Saxon, Anglican &
American. Once Families 'cross the Land would gather
at the pagan Solstice to mark the Closing-in of Winter.
In our Day Christmas is mark'd by my Lord **LAWSON**'s
buxom Daughter showing festive Fayre upon the eleck-
trickal Lantern, thus inducing **TUMESCENCE** in middle-
ag'd Men 'cross the same Land.

In the American Colonies, Carollers do forewarn Infants to be not Boisterous nor Tearful nor Petulant, telling that these are not fitting Virtues for the Arrival in Town of Saint NICHOLAS & imploring them to be good for the Sake of Goodness.

In England, 'tis customary to contemplate the most virtuous Christmas Rites, resolving to forego simple Turkey for fatty GOOSE, to perform charitable Acts in the Manner of WENCESLAS or to whittle Christmas Gifts from SCRAPS in the Manner of Miss Martha STEWART, before falling IDLE for Days afore the electrickal Nativity of Messrs MORECAMBE & WISE in a Miasma of Sprout-Smog.

England has produc'd the true Bards of the Christmas Season, viz. Messrs Chas. DICKENS & Nods. HOLDER. In their Honour I do propose the following Definitions:

Advent Calendar ⇸ *n.*
solemn retelling of the Story of our LORD'S Nativity thro' Chockolate

Christmas Day ⇸ *n.*
day 'pon which one receives Gifts one desires & Relatives one does NOT

Christmas Special ⇸ *n.*
seasonal Night-Soil; a festive Parp of the IDIOT-LANTERN

Christmas Tree ⇸ *n.*
lustrous Evergreen that, when hewn and domestickated,
becomes Pale & **BALD**

> *Also, that which ought to be Out-Side brought In-side by*
> *Germanick* **CONSORT***; bedeck'd by oft-faltering eleck-*
> *tronick* **CANDLES**

Cracker ⇸ *n.*
incendiary **DEVICE** requiring two Participants willing
to receive Brummagem Itemry, Hattage & comick
FLOTSAM

C Is For Cinema

The electronick Theatre is oft call'd the greatest new
Form of Art of the present **ERA**. 'Tis certainly the most
opulently fund'd of all Arts: for one never hears of a
Playwright paid twenty Million Guineas as Recompense
to compose a next Act, nor of a Poet who requir'd
seventy thousand Quills of India-Ink & a Spodeware
Vessel of colour-pars'd M&Ms in Order to pen a Sonnet.

Great Money does bring forth great Spectacle: and
with it does come the inevitable Retinue of great Folly &
great Acts of **VANITY**. Sufficient Bounty can lower the
finest Shakespearean Actor to a Role from a Child's
Paper Comick. A celebrated Actress may command vast
Chests of Treasure to perform in th'electronick Theatre,

yet her Face be so frozen by Mister **JENNER'S** patent Pox-Injection that said Performance is more like a Mask with working Eyes. Conversely a Player may garner fawning Notes of Praise as **AUTHENTICK**, which transpires to mean that he does brawl like a Stevedore & does ingest copious Laudanum in his Carriage 'pon the Set. I thus conclude that this much-vaunted Rawness is a Quality as undesirable in Acting as in a Pork **CHOP**.

Embolden'd with a sufficient Menagerie of Actors & a sufficient Provision of Gunpowder, the Cinema of today is content to dispense with **SCRIPT**. A cow-like Audience will watch a full Hour of Explosion in preference to a Minute of Plot. Yet a Folly persists that Actors do captivate the Masses when, in Truth, 'tis the Trickery of the Especial-Effeckts that do enchant, whilst the poor Actor does merely strut & berate 'gainst a Screen of Blue. Henceforward, the magick-lantern Wizardry of three Dimensions shall add Depth unto Productions that have been bless'd with none from the **PLOT**.

Herewith a series of Definitions & Aphorisms that shall soon come unto a Screen near thee:

Art House ⤳ *n.*
a cant Designation for foreign Film; measur'd in subtle Nuance of Plot or simple Quantity of Bubb-Flesh

Avatar ⤳ *n.*
Mister **CAMERON'S** blue-skinn'd dramatick Folly, present'd at a Cost of all the Treasures of the **AMERICAS**

Bereft of a Ticket to see Avatar at th'electronick Theatre, I daub myself with Woad & place stain'd Glass 'pon my Eyes to replickate it

BAFTAS ⇸ *n.*
cunning Trail of Red Carpet, laid to fool guileless English Actors in to believing that it does lead to **HOLLYWOOD**

Mister BEAN ⇸ *n.*
tragick Biography of a dumb-struck Imbecile, favour'd only due to the grave Cruelty of foreign Audiences

Bruno ⇸ *n.*
affeckted Habsburg **MOLLY** who assaults the Buttocks of Strangers to prove that Strangers do dislike Assaults 'pon their Buttocks

Cinematography ⇸ *n.*
invisible Art at which a Film may be consider'd the Best, without a single human Soul taking Notice

Dirty Dancing ⇸ *n.*
Mister **SWAYZE'S** licentious Cavort, at which Participants are said to have the Time of their Lives

Robert DOWNEY, Jr ⇸ *n.*
Gurning **HAM**, renown'd for being imprison'd doubly by a Suit of futuristick **ARMOUR** & by his own **DEVIANT** Tastes

Will FERRELL → *n.*
shouting colonial Mummer who incites consiſtent
Hilarity by portraying the same Person in his every Work

> *Other celebrated Mummers who do miſtake the noble*
> *Craft of Acting for the base Act of Shouting do include*
> *Messrs Jack* **BLACK**, *Benj.* **KINGSLEY** *& Samuel*
> **JACKSON**, *and withal Sicilian Hobgoblin Signor Al*
> **PACINO**

High School Musical → *n.*
a juvenile Jamboree of white-tooth'd **JOY**; & thus an
ORDEAL teſting the very Tolerance of its Audience

Lord of the Rings → *n.*
fantaſtickal Epic, ſtag'd in New Zealand: it takes as long
to Watch as that far Country takes to Visit

> *Wise Criticks should observe that* The Lord of the Rings *is*
> *no more than two Dwarves that set out on a lengthy Walk,*
> *later beset by scheming Phantasms & bracing* **SCENERY**

Love Acually → *n.*
Miſter Richard **CURTIS** does disguise great Voids of
PLOT by enacting them in the moſt pleasant of **HOMES**

Oscar → *n.*
gilded Cudgel that an Actor may use in Defence 'gainſt
his Fellows who have deliver'd similar Performances to
lesser Acclaim

Porn ⇸ *n.*
most base Depiction of the Act of Love, differ'd from
th'Everyday by twice the Number of Partners & half the
Quantity of **MERKIN**

Sequel ⇸ *n.*
second Rendition of a Film, compos'd if a Plot has not
been explor'd or a paying Audience has not been
exploited

Snakes on a Plane ⇸ *n.*
drama prais'd for the Directness of its **TITLE**; then
damn'd by the Directness of its **REVIEWS**

Star Wars ⇸ *n.*
wherein Mister Geo. **LUCAS** does squander Themes of
Buddhism, Chivalry & Mythologie 'pon **INFANTS**

> *'Know you that Master Luke* **SKYWALKER** *is a Cipher for*
> *an Homerick Hero's* **ODYSSEY**?' *'No, he is a mere* **DOLL**'

Oliver STONE ⇸ *n.*
Chronicler of Conspiracy; today more likely to die at the
Hands of a disappoint'd Audience than a Cabal of secret
Powers

D *is for* **DISNEY**

Dalek ⇸ *n.*
ironmonger'd Hobgoblin that imperils all CREATION
for up to five-and-forty Minutes at a TIME

Davos ⇸ *n.*
Helvetian Caravanserai where great Men whose
Commerce has made the World WORSE now talk loftily
of how to make the World BETTER

Dentistry ⇸ *n.*
Mouth-Doctoring; though practis'd on Teeth, it does in
fact tend unto the Needs of the MIND, viz. Vanity &
Cruelty

> *The Pursuit of Dentistry unfolds thus: 'Flush with*
> *Advances, I now demand that my Mouth should shine*
> *forth as if the very Gates of He'en were to open 'twixt my*
> *Lips.' 'Mister* AMIS, *you are now possess'd of a Rictus-Grin*
> *of whitest Alabaster.' 'Indeed, Sir, procur'd for but ten thou-*
> *sand* FLORINS *& a Month of* ANGUISH'

Deodorant ⇸ *n.*
Miasma that, when apply'd underarm in sufficient
Depth, is held by Primitives & English Youths to convey
Irresistibility

Derby ⇸ *n.*
localis'd Sporting JOUST whereupon Townsfolk do
funnel thro' Turnstiles to sing of their Neighbours'
Diseases, Parentage, &c

Destiny's Child ⇸ *n.*
comely Trio of Wenches who repeat Mrs
Wollstonecraft's Case for female Emancipation
while clad in saucy Under-Garments

Devil ⇸ *n.*
baleful Fiend who proffers Riches in exchange for Men's
Souls: a Task now undertaken by Mister Simon
Cowell

Diabetes ⇸ *n.*
Afflicktion of the Humours resulting from a man's
rightfull Love of **Liberty** becoming supplanted by Love
of **Banbury Cakes**

Disneyland ⇸ *n.*
America's earthly **Paradise**, otherwise stain'd by a
simple Mouse plotting with a grasping Scotch **Duck** &
his infernal Nephews

Doctor ⇸ *n.*
medickal Honorific, now bestow'd on Imposters such as
Oetker, Fox, Hook & Who

Donkey Sanctuary ⇸ *n.*
gilded Stable, built on Legacy & Sentiment; an Ass-Hole

Dope ⇸ *adj.*
Accolade indicating the Possession of admirable
Qualities; that which is not **Wack**

Doughnut ⇸ *n.*
Sugar'd Paſtry with a scant Middle that remedies the
same Condition in those that eat it

Driver ⇸ *n.*
convivial Conversationaliſt & sender of Text who, inci-
dentally, does pilot a Ton of motoris'd **STEEL**

Dubai ⇸ *n.*
Bedouin Conjuring-Trick whereby gilt Taps do diſtrackt
from the sorry Disappearance of **LIBERTY**

Dyson ⇸ *n.*
miraculous mechanickal Barrel that both performs
household Chores & is the sole Evidence of British
Manufackturing **INGENUITY**

D Is For *Daily Mail*

The *Daily Mail* is the moſt consulted Publickation for
Britain's Women. Herein the fairer Sex may read of the
moſt grievous Ends that await any Female who dares
enter the Workplace, for unto the *Daily Mail* a Woman
who does possess a Career is as vexatious as a Prussian
who does possess a **MUSKET**.

Likewise the *Mail* does issue shrill Pronouncements
'pon everyday Sundries that may cause a Cancer, or
indeed cure it. Depending 'pon the Day of Reading, one

may discover that a humble Tincture of Tea does bring forth vile Tumours, does proteckt the Body from them, or, most oft, does **BOTH**. It does follow an equally fork'd Path 'pon Matters foreign, for it warns that the most diabolickal Fate is to be govern'd by French-Men, yet the most desirable Prize is to win a Home in France.

The *Daily Mail* does invite its hot-head'd Readers to Have Your Say; an injunction that brings forth opinion-ated **BILE** like a Barber-Surgeon lancing a **BOIL**.

Hearby I do have my **SAY**:

Diana ↦ *n.*
sainted Princess whose every Words were venerated, save her Pleas for Privacy

Richard LITTLEJOHN ↦ *n.*
mob-rousing Falstaff whose discourses 'gainst Mollies & Sodomy may be Windows unto his hidden **DESIRES**

Prize Draw ↦ *n.*
covetous Lottery whereby one favour'd Reader may obtain a Cottage, be voted an annual Pension & thus escape the lower Orders

D Is For Drugs

The most contentious Variety of Physick is referred to as Drugs.

A civilised Society does have a rightful Place & proper Usage for divers Drugs: Laudanum for medickall Necessity, Æther for the Dentist's **ART**, Snuff for the thirsty-nostrill'd Gentleman, e'en Messrs **PRINGLE'S** extrud'd Potato-Suns to enliven a Party by their unstoppable **POPPING**. In British Society, the rightful Place does appear to be in the Lives of Musicians, the Estates of the Poor & the Pages of News-Papers.

There is much hot-blooded Debate as to whether Drugs do dull or stimulate the Person. Their phantasmagorick Effeckts certainly do fall far beyond the poor Jackanapes who do actually **INGEST** the Drugs. Drugs do have the most deathly deleterious Effeckt 'pon any Person who **SPEAKS** of them. An Innocent who is lur'd into the Debate o'er Drugs will emerge either as a Libertine or as a **PRIG**. Those Troubadours & Scriveners who would enthuse upon Drugs submit themselves unto the grave risk of **NINCOMPOOPERY**. Consider the cautionary Tales of:

> Jumping Caucasian Mister Woodrow **HARRELSON**, who professes great Dedickation unto Hemp Rope-Makery yet would ignite & ingest the very Fruits of the Rope-Maker's Art;

Lewdly leather'd Myſtick Miſter Jas. **MORRISON**, who proclaim'd himself Monarch of all Lizards;

Raw-bon'd Scare-Crow Miſter Igworth **POP**, who did grievously abrade his Breaſt with a Decanter 'pon the very **STAGE** with his divers Stooges;

And good Doctor of Letters Miſter Hunter **THOMPSON**, who took both to brandishing Piſtols & to wearing yellow'd Eye-Glasses in the Manner of Cockney Chariot-Merchant Miſter Francis **BUTCHER**.

I have observed a scientifick Ratio for the moſt ill-fam'd of Drugs: those which do cause frenzie'd Palsy in the Nation's Dance-Halls shall do the same in the Nation's **LEGISLATIVE CHAMBERS**.

Of those who do partake in Drugs, there is scant Sign of Intelleckt, but far greater Sign of Ingenuity. The Youths of Britain who show no Aptitude for the Teaching of Miſter Robert **BOYLE'S** Chemiſtry do yet show great Ingenuity in Search of intoxickating Herbs & Physick. Similarly they show remarkable Proficiency for Fractions, able to divide any Avoirdupois Quantity in to Quartos, Eighths & e'en Sixteenths of an Ounce. The Mind that does exhibit sufficient experimentall Nature to partake of Physick for Horses & Food for Plants, or to ingeſt thro' Cavities **NASAL & RECTAL** might yet earn a Berth in the Royall **SOCIETY**.

While Criticks charge that Drugs bend the Mind, they

certainly do bend the English Language in to a most perverse Form. His Majesty King **HENRY VIII** & French *Roi* **LOUIS XVI** are both press'd in to Service as Units of Measurement. Merchants do hawk their Wares with bawdy Catcalls of 'Art thou *sort'd,* Good Sir Geezer? For I shall hit thee upwards.' And Mister **HARRELSON'S** Hemp is known by such a Panoply of Monikers, viz. Black, Grass, Resin, Tea, Weed, &c., that it does outfox the cataloguing Lexicographer as surely as it bamboozles the pursuing Bow Street **RUNNER**.

For those who do hunger for Drug Definitions in the Manner of Mister **JONES**, herewith I do have what you **NEED**:

Cannabis ⇸ *n.*
most producktive Plant from which is sourc'd stout Rope & Burlap, Palliatives, Nick-Names, herbal Cigarillos & moral **PANICKS**

Cocaine ⇸ *n.*
potent Snuff that does invest the Partaker with th'Illusion of Omnipotence & his Membrum the Reality of Impotence

Crack ⇸ *n.*
a Brigand's Confection; its Taste inspiring grievous Felony, thus generally presum'd to be most **MOREISH**

Drug Dealer ⇸ *n.*
Part Smuggler, Footpad & Merchant, diſtinguish'd by his ceremonial Uniform of puff'd Top-Coat & capp'd Hat

Ecſtacy ⇸ *n.*
turbulent Tablet, much associat'd with the quaint Fashion for nocturnal Barn-Dances in Fields about the Metropolis

Head-Shop ⇸ *n.*
dismal Merchant who sources his Wares from the far Edges of Legality & his Cuſtom from the far Reaches of Reſpectability

Ketamine ⇸ *n.*
Physick, which in England is generally giv'n to Horses, but in Scotland supports the capering Youths

Medickall Marijuana ⇸ *n.*
Designation wherein the Law of the Spanish Colony California does afflict certain of the Populace with GLAUCOMA

Meow Meow ⇸ *n.*
Plant-Food sequeſter'd for Intoxication: it can both summon forth Fauna from the Earth & place People into it

Prescription ⇸ *adj.*
class of Physick favour'd both by the Law & by dissolute

Celebrities: created to cure Malady; consum'd to induce Madness

Rehab ⇸ *n.*
State of Contrition through which Knaves are first wean'd from their Appetites & then absolv'd of their Sins by the Press-Men

Stoned ⇸ *adj.*
to be Red of Eye, Slow of Wit, Lethargick of Countenance, Hungry of Belly & Subjeckt of much American cinematick Comedy

E *is for* Ecover

Early Adopter ⇸ *n.*
he who would purchase Mister Jas. **WATT'S** first Steam-Engine before it does e'en **WORK** as Proof of his high Modernity

Eastenders ⇸ *n.*
Troupe of fabrickated Cockney-Oiks who do parade their Woes before the Publick with the Regularity of the Clock

Ecover ⇸ *n.*
miraculous Tincture that makes Dirt vanish from the Garments, **GUILT** vanish from the Soul, and **GOLD** vanish from the Pocket

English Breakfast ⇸ *n.*
Exhibit of all the Provisions that England has to offer, quarter'd in a Skillet & preserv'd in Tallow

Espresso ⇸ *n.*
Italianate Coffee-Tincture brew'd in Strength 'twixt Beverage & Narcotick, so as to induce St **VITUS'S** Dance in him who drinks it

Estate-Agent ⇸ *n.*
a Trickster who claims that Homes are veritable Treasure-Chests e'en when his own Business is an empty **CUPBOARD**

Eton ⇸ *n.*
publick School of such high Renown that its Pupils are sanction'd to govern the Country during their Holidays

Eurosport ⇢ *n.*
bereft of all Funding, a Channel for Sports so **OBSCURE**
that Participants oft out-number Viewers

Eurovision ⇢ *n.*
Molly-House of Enthusiastick **MINSTRELS** from divers
States, from Muscovy to Prussia & Savoy

Evening Standard ⇢ *n.*
worthless Handbill informing Londoners whether they
are to be stabb'd & what the Children of the Gentry do
wear

Exam ⇢ *n.*
a blunt Test of Aptitude, in which three Years of
IGNORANCE is cramm'd in to three Hours of **SILENCE**

E Is For England

*In which yr. humble Author does travel o'er divers Counties
Palatine, Ridings, Parishes & Stations-of-Service to chronickle
his Mother-Country.*

On Occasion, it may be incumbent 'pon a Gentle-Man
to leave the great Wen of London and embark on a
Journey unto the Provinces of England. Such an
Itinerary should prove a most instrucktive Record of the
Nation; each Destination adding a further Patch-Work
to the dun-colour'd Quilt of Britannia.

I hasten'd to procure Tickets for the departing Coach at the Victoria Coaching-Inn. Most surpris'd to note that I would not travel 'pon a Coach-and-Six or Phaeton but in a white Behemoth livery'd **NATIONAL EXPRESS**. Fortuitously the Coach had the employ of a Privy-Closet, nestling betwixt Seat & Steps. Within the Closet was a Jakes awash with blue-hue'd Liquor, from which I saw fit not to sup. Viands & Vittles were quartermaster'd from Mister **KLIX'S** Patent Glass & Iron Armoire that, for a Pittance of Coins, would spout forth sparkling Water, hot Tea or sustaining Broth, oft in the same Cupful.

Such sluggish Pace was made from Victoria unto the Swiss Cottage that I believ'd the Distance-Markers on the Highway to demarcate not Miles but Hours travell'd.

Within a few short Hours I had forded the Motor-Way Five-and-Twenty, a Macadam'd Moat seemingly construct'd by Londonfolk to prevent the Ingress of cheap Ale & Lodgings in to the Capital. 'Twas a Moment of great Stillness, for all the Coaches & Chariots did sit **UNMOV'D**.

I had arriv'd at the Home Counties, the most idyllick Corners of England, whose genteel People have much to teach us of Manners. I had hop'd to encounter aged marital Exemplars **TERRY & JUNE**, or to see divers Crimes & Misdemeanours harrow'd up in the Village of **MIDSOMER**, yet to no Avail.

At Essex I fear'd I had been stricken by grievous Catarackts, for I no longer saw in the same chromatick

Register: all Carriages were white, all Hair was straw-yellow and the Faces of the People were deepest **MAHOGANY**. Abutting Essex lies Suffolk, a County most notable for being due south of Norfolk. The County of Norfolk itself is platitudinous in all Senses: most of the Land is Water & the highest man-made Structure is Mister Stephen **FRY**.

My Coachman eschew'd the rightful Coaching-Stop for a barren Settlement nam'd a **SERVICE STATION**. Service came there none: 'tis merely a cover'd Latrine that all may visit before procuring motoring Sundries. While all who visit a Service Station do piss forth **TOGETHER**, the Dining-Halls do separate Men by **CLASS**: the middling Sort have Costa Coffee, th'infernal Little Chef for the Footman.

My next Destination was the North of England, fam'd for its great Neighbourliness. Indeed its Inhabitants are oft found in the Homes of their Neighbours, availing themselves of Cash, Chattels, Plate, &c. Near Manchester, garrulous comick Father-and-Son Messrs Peter & Vernon **KAY** do habitually declare themselves to be Denizens of **BOLTON**, which serves as a Warning not to enter that Town. I thus assay its southern Twin to be **SLOUGH**, a Borough already so characteris'd by Messrs John **BETJEMAN** & David **BRENT** that 'tis now both unnecessary & unwise to visit it.

Further North still lies the City of Newcastle, a Polis that has given the Nation such Figures as Bee-moniker'd

Druid **STING**, Miss Cheryl **COLE**, Messrs **ANT & DEC** and lachrymose Clown Miſter Paul **GASCOIGNE**, yet has ne'er formally apologis'd. The Dialeckt of the people of Newcaſtle is moſt low and barbarous: replete with Terms such as **HINNY, PET & HAWAY**, it sounds to English Ears like a Man who has swallow'd a bak'd **POTATO**.

Hereunder some Notables of England:

Briſtol ⤳ *n.*
weſterly Port, built 'pon Slavery, now support'd on three Pillars of Wildlife Daguerreotypery, Clay Puppetry & Traffick of **HEMP**

> *Alternatively, in Weſtern England, a Seaport; in Eaſtern London, a vulgar Term for a Lady's* **BUBB**

Brummie ⤳ *n.*
of a Person, to be from the Heart of England; of an Accent, to ſpeak from the Nose of England

Cambridge ⤳ *n.*
blaſted Fenland City, home unto Britain's greateſt scientifick Luminaries, also to Sir Clive **SINCLAIR**

Cornwall ⤳ *n.*
precarious Promontory of Rock, consider'd barbarous eſpecially when invad'd by the Holiday-Making Gentry

> *The Cornishman is the moſt extraordinary Beaſt. A red-head'd Rouſtabout of a Man, once rightly confin'd to*

Tin Mines, the Cornishman is now free to ride Surf
mounted athwart a Gang-Plank whilst cursing Visitors
who make the perilous Journey unto his County in a
Language seemingly patch'd from Breton, Folk-Jigs & a
Surfeit of the Letter R. The Cornishman's Diet may account
for his cholerick Manner, comprising as it does Flagons of
Apple-Cider & a crimp'd Half-Moon of lowly Chuck &
beastly Swede

Durham ⇻ *n.*
diminutive City wherein money'd Scholars of lesser
Intellect may half-close their Eyes and believe themselves to be in **OXFORD**

Manchester ⇻ *n.*
red-brick'd Hades, in which are found Old Trafford &
Coronation Street, both vulgar Stages for strutting
Performers

Scouser ⇻ *n.*
a Mersey-man who does regale you with Tales of his
Warm Heart & Good Humour unto the very Point at
which he does **ASSAULT** you

The Scouser is most easy to distinguish, for he shall
regale you without Prompting 'pon the divers Virtues
of his People & Home-Town, which he has left and
unto which shall never return. In a Marvel of
Geometry worthy of Euclid, fully eight-in-ten

Households in Liverpool were once adjacent to those of the Beatles

Whitstable ⇸ *n.*
bleak Mudflat where the rich & voluble of the Capital briefly flee the Misery of their Wealth to live in **HUTS**

Yorkshire ⇸ *n.*
largest County in the Land, yet still not large enough to accommodate its Inhabitants' swoll'n Sense of their own **IMPORTANCE**

> *When provok'd into great Ire, the Yorkshireman issues forth his reknown'd War Cry: 'How Much?'*

As an Addendum unto this Survey of the Nation, I must share Reports of inhabit'd Land unto the North of Britain. Intrepid Voyagers have call'd this barren Granite Outcrop Scotland. 'Tis most vexatious to speculate of its People, for Scotland's most notable Sons are: Fictitious, in the Manner of Mister Melvin **GIBSON'S** eviscerated Barbarian Mister Wm. **WALLACE**; long since fled in Exile 'gainst the Excise, in the Manner of Mister **CONNERY**, or designat'd as British, in the Manner of Mister **BROWN**.

Venturing that some might indeed inhabit this Scot-Land, I would offer a conciliatory Definition of the Scotchman thus:

Scotsman → *n.*
a Man condemn'd to Live in perpetual Cold from the North Sea & in perpetual Resentment 'gainſt the English

E Is For Europe

The aſtute Observer of England will perceive that there is **LAND** across the English Channel & North Sea. Close Inſpection does reveal the Land to be inhabit'd by foreign Souls, so-call'd Europeans. These Europeans do then fissiparate in to divers Principalities, Archbishopricks, Margravines, Duchies, Elecktorates & Republicks, both for the Amusement of the Englishman & for the Vexation of the Cartographer.

One may assay many Truths about the Charackter of Europe from its myriad Languages. The coldly precise Teuton has fully six Words for 'The' yet merely one for 'I Thank You'. The Dutchman has maſter'd Fluency in the English tongue, for ſpok'n Dutch does sound as if one had thruſt a Stick down the Throat of a **DOG** & bade it talk. Italian is oft suppos'd to be the Language of Love, for those that do ſpeak it are in perpetual Pursuit of others' **WIVES**.

One fanciful Supposition ſtates that the British & the Europeans share common Anceſtry & are merely divided by scant Sea-Channels. They cite Commonality of Names: a Miſter **BROWN** may derive from Meinherr

Braun, Monsieur **Lebrun** or Signor **Bruno**; likewise Mister Peter **Andre** may equally be claim'd by any Nation. There is certainly a History of Exchange 'twixt Britain & Europe: 'tis a Land whence we did take our Kings, then did take our Battles, now in which we take Holiday and e'en whence we take Leadership.

Indeed such Proximity to foreign Lands does permit the Englishman to use Europe as a Kind of moral Looking-Glass in which he may see his particular Differences magnify'd & his own Faults reflect'd.

Herewith the principal Observations from that very Looking-Glass:

Amsterdam ⇢ *n.*
City reclaim'd from the Sea: now so immoral that it may return there due to God's **Wrath**

> *Dutchmen are grown awful* **Tall**, *thus suffering them to breathe in th'inevitable Event of the Breaching of the Dykes. The Dutchman, so in Thrall unto pornographick Pamphlets & narcotick Herbs, must balance his lewd Life by denying himself other Pleasures. Thus no Food is permitted in the entire Dutch Republick more elaborate than a Sandwich of toasted Ham & Cheese*

Andorra ⇢ *n.*
minor Ravine 'twixt France & Spain in to which much untax'd Money has roll'd

Austria ⇸ *n.*
Sprightly Mountain Republick, much like Germany if not more so

Basque ⇸ *n.*
Language compos'd of Letters J&X; Hell for Speakers, very Heaven for **SCRABBLE-PLAYERS**

Belgium ⇸ *n.*
officious Customs-Union; a doughty Bastion of Defence 'gainst the rising Cultures of 'Can-Do' & 'No-Problem'

Europe ⇸ *n.*
various Lands outwith Great Britain, wherein **FOOD** is invariably **BETTER** but Manners are much **WORSE**

European Parliament ⇸ *n.*
Chamber built for picking Arguments with Foreigners, thus a Temple to the most naturall of European Instincts

Eurosceptic ⇸ *adj.*
to doubt the Legitimacy of politickal Europe: at Extremes, to doubt the very Existence of Europe

The Parliament of Europe does furnish its harshest Criticks with fine Offices & Sinecures, each a Vantage-Point from which they may bite the Hand that does feed them

Eurostar ⇢ *n.*
continental Carriage, so asham'd to link England unto
France that it does so 'neath the Ground

France ⇢ *n.*
barbarous Hexagon that serves no Purpose save to
narrow the Channel & refleckt the superior Virtues of
ENGLAND

> *Visitors do observe that France's Super-Markets contain*
> *some ten Varieties of Mustard yet not one Variety of*
> **COURTESY**

Germany ⇢ *n.*
Prussian & Rhineish Electorates whose Tradition of
Barbarism is now limited to serving Cake & hard-boil'd
Eggs at Breakfast

Greece ⇢ *n.*
Land in which the noble Athenians did establish
DEMOCRACY, PHILOSOPHY & CIVILISATION, then
subsequently down'd Tools

Iceland ⇢ *n.*
now Penurious volcanick Outcrop, rul'd over by Bedlamite
Queens Bjork **GUÐMUNDSDÓTTIR** & Kerry **KATONA**

> *There is much Speculation that, fac'd with national*
> *Bankruptcy, Misses* **GUÐMUNDSDÓTTIR & KATONA**
> *conspir'd to burn down the Island for Insurance Purposes*

Ireland ⇝ *n.*
damp Island, rousing great Passion in its native Sons,
moſt of whom do then leave it

> *Ireland is fam'd for its many musickal Luminaries, moſt*
> *notable of which is portentous Quartet U2, led by hectoring*
> *Statesman and occasional Singer Miſter* **BONO**. *Others of*
> *Note are comely Maiden Miss* **THIN-LIZZY** *& ranting*
> *Minſtrel-Lad Maſter Sinead* **O'CONNOR**, *presum'd to be a*
> *Son of antient Gaelick Comick Miſter Tom* **O'CONNOR**

Italy ⇝ *n.*
boot-shap'd Kingdom: its Citizenry tends towards
Lawlessness; its Government does explain **WHY**

> *Italy is such a singular fighting Nation that its Ensign is*
> *the White-Flag. One may discern all there is to know of*
> *Italy within five minutes of Arrival at its borders. Its*
> *Cuſtoms-Officers, more concern'd with the Artifice of*
> *Appearance than the Adminiſtration of good*
> *Government, do wear shaded Glasses. They do but two*
> *Things well: the Stamping of Documents and the*
> *Wearing of blue* **SHIRTS**

Luxembourg ⇝ *n.*
dwarfish Statelet whose very Name, like that of
LIECHTENSTEIN, does o'erlap its actual Borders

Majorca ⇀ *n.*
Isle of Tranquillity, where Relaxation is thwarted by the Twin-Head'd **HYDRA** of white **SOCKS** and Prussian **VOICES**

Poland ⇀ *n.*
Slavonick Land whose Sons have master'd the plumbing Arts, tho' due to Surfeits of Cabbage & Sausage, not the culinary Arts

Russia ⇀ *n.*
vast eastern Stage, upon which cruel History does rehearse its every Form of **TYRANNY**

Spain ⇀ *n.*
Hispanick Land in which the Natives do dine ungodly **LATE**, to avoid the brutish Manners of the visiting **ENGLISH**

Switzerland ⇀ *n.*
discreet Canton concealing its Wealth behind foreboding Mountains & Laws so that its vexatious Neighbours might not notice

E Is For Exercise

The Maintenance of Health is a simple Matter of Cause & Effeckt, whereby the Intake of Foodstuffs does balance the Expenditure of bodily Effort. Yet today, coddl'd with bounteous Hula Hoops & a reclin'd Chair, Intake & Expenditure would soon swell a sitting Englishman into a human Tribute to Miss Peppa **PIG**.

Hence the modern Man muſt contrive **EXERCISES** to ſtir his sullen Form. It is a far from dignify'd Spectacle.

No Man, save one pursued by **TIGERS**, should run. Yet that explains why he does. He who pursues **EXERCISE** does sacrifice his Dignity to his Mortality. He runs like a Man in abject Fear of his Life from the inevitable Fate of **DECREPITUDE**.

Politicians such as Messrs **CLINTON**, **BROWN**, **CAMERON & SARKOZY**, who do wish to seem Virile & possess'd of Parts & **BOTTOM**, do run amidſt a Phalanx of Guards-Men in full Purview of the Press-Men. This cant Diſplay of Vitality, nam'd **JOGGING**, does imply that the Electorate might well compel Candidates to perform Acts of Tumbling & Jumping-Jacks to secure Votes, or that one might as well replace the Huſtings with a Vaulting-Horse or **TRAMPOLINE**.

Should a Man prevail in his Pursuit of the damn'd Exercise, his Abdomen shall contort in to a Six-Pack, that is to say, a Carapace more suited unto a **TURTLE**, & he shall have many Anecdotes with which to regale his Fellows on the Topick of injur'd Knees, tiresome Heart-Beats & elaſtickated **TIGHTS**.

Likewise there is no dignify'd Form of **DRESS** for Exercise.

Swaddled in the Fleece of a Track-Suit **TROUSER**, a

Man looks like a gigantick **BABY**. When clad in artificed Raiments that do shine as Tallow-Oil 'pon Water & do 'wick' Perſpiration away from the body, no Man should be admitted to a Coffee-House, Dining-Club nor to polite Society. Moſt grievous of all are the Offſpring of the middling Sort, clad in cotton Tabards labell'd with their University or Workplace, viz. 'I toil for Messrs **ERNST & YOUNG'S** Counting-House & do run at their Beheſt 'pon the Week-end', or 'I did partake in fully three Years of ſtudy at th'eſteem'd University of Oxford yet squander'd that Time playing at Lacrosse in the Manner of a small **NAVAJO-CHILD**'.

Indeed, the Englishman is ill-suited to Exercise. Note how the moſt potent Forms of Exercise are all branded with foreign provenance: **LA** Fitness, Swiss Ball, Russian Kettle-Bell, for any such Activity daub'd with an English Name would suggeſt a slovenly, **SUET-FILL'D** Stillness.

Herewith some common, if not effickacious, Terms of **EXERCISE**:

Boxercise ⇢ *n.*
debas'd Version of the pugiliſtick Arts where a Lady may partake of the Exercise of a Fighter, but not of the certain **DEATH**

Cardio ⇢ *adj.*
that which does ſtir & aggravate the Heart-Beat, viz.

Running, Pedalling, hearing News of a further Series of *Jonathan* CREEK

Crunches ⇸ *pl.*
whereby a Man does curl up 'pon the Floor in the vain
Hope that he shall emerge anew as he does unfurl
himself

Gun Show ⇸ *n.*
a Peacock-like Diſplay of swollen Biceps & shrunken
Modeſty

Gymnasium ⇸ *n.*
an inverted Work-House that People do PAY to enter &
therein undergo Servitude

Jumping-Jacks ⇸ *n.*
unruly Jump where the four Limbs are flung HITHER &
YON; it both raises the Heart-Beat & opens the
Fundament

Personal Trainer ⇸ *n.*
Manservant of Vanity, paid in theory to Inſtruct 'pon
Exercises, but in practice to replace the Resolve of his
Maſter

Pilates ⇸ *n.*
a fearsome Combine of Strings & Pulleys that contorts
People in to Health; a Gallows for the Living

Sit-Ups ⇸ *n.*
unsightly Contracktion of the Abdomen; perform'd
once to don a Pair of **HOSE**, perform'd one hundred
Times for **EXERCISE**

Sportacus ⇸ *n.*
infantile Viking Jumping-Jack who does compel the
slovenly Youth of England unto **ACTIVITIE**

Virgin Active ⇸ *n.*
a Gymnasium in which slovenly People are compell'd to
Exercise by the grinning Spectre of Sir Richard
BRANSON

Yoga ⇸ *n.*
ſtretching Exercise, learn'd from Hindoo Sages who
renounce the material World, yet practis'd by the
Wealthy 'pon expensive **MATS**

F *is for* FACELIFT

Facelift ⇸ *n.*
remarkable Masque of Youth where aged Flesh does
Migrate discreetly unto the Hinterland of th'Ears &
Neck

> *There is great Sport to be had in observing senescent
> Ladies of the Americkan Colonies for Signs of Faceliftery,
> chief of which is a tighten'd Rictus of the Face, as if a
> Masque had replac'd once-human Flesh. Miss Madonna*
> **CICCONE** *does thus appear to be a Guest at a Venetian
> Masquerade at all times, or indeed to be an antient Relick
> collected by Sir Horace* **WALPOLE**

Family Fortunes ⇸ *n.*
smirking Farmhand Master Vernon **KAY** offers
Redemption unto Kinfolk bless'd with neither Wealth
nor **TALENT**

Farmers' Market ⇸ *n.*
perverse Exchange where the money'd Interest do
happily trade a **CWT** of Silver-Coin for a Carrot of good
Provenance

Farrow & Ball ⇸ *n. pl.*
duo of domestick Wraiths, who besiege the Walls of a
Home with divers Dun & Moss Mercury-Paints

> *The middling Sort will gladly expend copious Guineas 'pon
> the Daubery of Messrs* **FARROW & BALL** *until their*

Feminism → *n.*
Credo holding Women to be equal; advocat'd ſtridently
by Puritan Academicks & miſtakenly by Dancers aſtride
Poles

Feng Shui → *n.*
Chinaman's Art of Furniture-Moving, recently elevated
unto the Status of a **Religion**

Fileshare → *vb.*
to exchange Content musickal, literal & cinematick
without a Farthing pass'd unto Playwright or Scrivener:
a capital **Offence**

Flatscreen → *adj.*
moſt desir'd Format of Idiot-Lantern; a grand Portrait-
Frame for Households devoid of all **Art**

Fly → *adj.*
that which is deem'd Excellent, thus

'Miſter **Hargreaves**, *I hail yr. Invention of the Spinny-
Jenny to be moſt* **Fly***'*

Focus-Group → *n.*
Folly whereby a Merchant pretends to get closer to his
Cuſtomer by **Spying** on him through smok'd Glass

The Focus-Group is a mighty Sieve for Ideas: it does catch & isolate all that is Original. Scraps of discarded Opinion that do pass through its Mesh can be form'd in to a passable Manifesto for Government

Frequent Flyer → *n.*
a Man whose Esteem derives from how often he does leave the Country; oft to the secret Delight of his Compatriots

Fundamentalist → *n.*
one who applies unto daily Life all the Truths of the Torah, Bible & Koran, save those concerning Love & Mercy

F Is For Fashion

The Dandy has down the Ages been a Creature of publick Amusement, a person deserving the Publick's Stares & not their Emulation. Fashion itself is so barbarous that it must be chang'd each Season. Yet today Fashion has leach'd out towards the Masses. A lowly Manufactory Girl may acquire the self-same Raiments as a celebrated Actress from As Seen 'Pon Screen; while Scandinavian Seamstresses Messrs **HENNES & MAURITZ** do endeavour to replickate the Garb of the Gentry with an Industriousness that does border 'pon the epic.

The poxlike Spread of Fashion does mean that a Person's Clothes are now an accepted Topick of Conversation & Discourse. A Person may be judg'd by his Garmentry as if the Shirt-Pocket is a Window unto the SOUL. Learn'd News-Papers & Publick Prints do employ Fashion Correspondents; Scriveners whose Erudition might be best deploy'd to administer Learning or give a Sermon 'pon the Trinity, yet is squander'd in writing Discourses about the length of a Trouser-Leg, or issuing Barbs such as:

By GOD, *is that Monsieur* MONTGOLFIER'S *tiny Balloon athwart a length of Willow? No, 'tis Miss Lily* COLE.

At the basest Level of Signor DANTE'S Inferno sits a Creature call'd Fashion-Blogger, one who accosts Strangers in the Street to interrogate them on the Provenance of their Garments, as if a polite Yeoman should ever disclose the Choice or Mercery of his Shifts with a lowly Street-Etcher.

I shall thus endeavour to issue forth my own Correspondence 'pon Fashion. Herewith my Proclamations for the Season:

An enlighten'd Prince would legislate an upper Age for the Wearing of fleec'd Raiments & Suits of the TRACK

Bedlamite Harlequin Lady GAGA *is oft dress'd as Mister Abe.* DARBY'S *Iron-Bridge*

The Fashion for the Dandy is to ſtride around London dress'd as a Timber-Jack, wielding a Man-Bag in place of an **AXE**

The Dandy, reſplendent in his check'd Shirt, resembles not a ſtout Hudson Bay Timber-Jack but a **TABLE-CLOTH**

The Model's Figure: to the Magazines, 'Bless'd with good Conſtitution, I dine as I please', to the Porcelain, a daily **PURGATIVE**

And herewith my Definition of the many Brands & Styles of Fashion:

BODEN ⇸ *n.*
purveyors by Appointment to the lower Gentry of the national Coſtume of **FULHAM**

On Sight of well-heel'd Hordes clad in Miſter **BODEN'S** *Raiments, the poor Natives of Cornwall may deteƈt an Invasion of their Land as surely as Natives of the American Colonies did when eſpying great Phalanxes of Red-Coats*

Ralph LAUREN ⇸ *n.*
cant Mercer who peddles the Style of Life of New England, ſtripp'd of Paul **REVERE**, Musketry & Revolution

Levi's ⇸ *n.*
Overalls sewn for a Collier, proffer'd to a dandy Youth, then bought by Mister Jeremy **CLARKSON**

Ben SHERMAN ⇸ *n.*
Footpad's Costumier, Purveyor of Broadcloth to Street-Urchins

Ugg Boots ⇸ *n.*
carv'd from the Feet of a **WOMBLE**, thus a grave Cruelty in the Name of Fashion

Vivienne WESTWOOD ⇸ *n.*
derang'd Seamstress, held to be th'offspring of Miss Helena **BONHAM-CARTER** & Mister Ronald **MCDONALD**

F Is For food

The Englishman practises a great Deception on himself in the Kitchen.

He believes he does dine on Home-Cook'd Vittles, dutifully following the Precepts laid down by Culinary Deity Miss Delia **SMITH** & capacious-tongu'd Cockney Master James **OLIVER**. He gads Hither & Yon about the Farmers' Market in the Manner of Marie Antionette, feigning great Interest in the historickal Biography of this Cheese-Truckle or the Welfare of that Sausage, fully deluded that the Boar or Sow contain'd therein was lull'd to Sleep by Harpsichord-Musick & then tickl'd unto Death.

Yet the Truth does lie somewhere different. For the Englishman is a creature of Convenience, partaking his Custard from Mister **BIRD**, his Fish from Capt. **BIRDSEYE** & his Scratchings from Mister **PORKY**. The scientifick Ingenuity of Messrs **BOYLE & FARADAY** is today most likely to be deploy'd in Quests to flavour a Potato-Crisp with Porto-Wine or to adumbrate Mister Benj. **FRANKLIN'S** Cheese of Philadelphia. For the true-heart'd Englishman the cant Term 'Locally Sourc'd' does mean that which is procured from the local **MOTOR-GARAGE**.

Scant Wonder that Parsley is the rightful Herb of England, for merely one Sprig may guise a grocer-bought Repast as the Fruits of one's own Kitchen Labours.

Herewith that which does fill the Basket & swell the Spirit of the Englishman:

Baby Bel ⇢ *n.*
Dutchman's Cheese, preserv'd in waxen Spheres to aid Carriage, Storage & doubtless Ignition; indeed, all Aspects save Eating

Chocolate Orange ⇢ *n.*
Mister **TERRY'S** fearsome citrus Cannonball, equally apt in a Fusillade of Shell & Round-Shot or as an Easter-Gift

Coca-Cola ⇸ *n.*
patent Syrup, held at various Times both to contain the
potent Elixir of the Coca-Leaf & to teach the World to
sing

Coco Pops ⇸ *n.*
whereby a Monkey does defecate into a Child's Milk-
Bowl & then sing Doggerels of its infamous **DEED**

Cracker ⇸ *n.*
Miſter **JACOBS'** dry Water-Biscuit, ingeniously prim'd to
explode 'pon Contaƈt with soft Cheese

Creme Egg ⇸ *n.*
fantaſtickal Rendering of Almighty **GOD'S** Creation in
Cocoa, Filigree & **GLUE**

Crunchie ⇸ *n.*
great Artifice whereby Machinery & Alchemy do dare
to replickate Nature's own **HONEY-COMBE**

Curly Wurly ⇸ *n.*
Lattic'd Cocoa-Bar eaten in the Present, yet enjoy'd in
the Paſt: 'I recall when Curly Wurly was as mighty as an
OAK', &c.

Dairylea ⇸ *n.*
armour-plated Triangle of whitish Salt-Paſte, once
believ'd to be a diſtant Relative of **CHEESE**

Danone ⇸ *n.*
French Conspiracy for the Curation of Ill Humours,
Ague, Bloody Flux & St Anthony's Fire by Means of
sour'd Milk

Fish Fingers ⇸ *n. pl.*
maize-encrusted Appendages of a fabricated Sea-
Creature, then hawk'd by a fabricated Sea-Captain

Lindt ⇸ *n.*
a Vatican of Cocoa, each Pronouncement replete with
Sin, wrapp'd in Gold & seal'd with golden Bells

Muesli ⇸ *n.*
divers Seeds, Chaff & Grain thought to fortify the
Helvetian; better us'd as Fortification for his Mountain-
Chalet

Ryvita ⇸ *n.*
girth-Comptroll Biscuit: its drab Plasterboard Taste may
be mask'd by great Divots of cream'd Cheese

Snickers ⇸ *n.*
Nut-festoon'd Cudgel, sold as a brazen Ploy to entice
Men unto Chockolate

Special K ⇸ *n.*
Husks of Rice, four-and-ten Bowlfuls of which compel
the Eater to don a scarlet Dress or Denim-Britches of
inferior Size

Turkey Twizzlers ⇸ *n.*
Poultry Truncheon, possess'd of scant nutritional Value
yet great entertainment Value for it so irks Jamie
OLIVER

Walkers Crisps ⇸ *n.*
jug-ear'd Marionette Mister **LINEKER'S** Plot to pervert
England's Potato-Crop with dastardly foreign
Adulterations

G *is for* GRAVY

Gatwick ⤳ *n.*
Godforsaken Port of Embarkation that claims to be Part of London yet is found in the coastal County of **SUSSEX**

GCSE ⤳ *n.*
Exam ritual where the Results show **GENIUS**, the political Commentators show Spoon-fed **MILKSOPS** & the News-Papers show Comely Maidens

Frank GEHRY ⤳ *n.*
celebrated Architect whose sole Talent is to enwrap a Building in metallick Filigree, like a roast'd **CHICKEN**

Geordie ⤳ *adj.*
coming from Northumberland, a Province so distant that English is understood merely as a Sequence of **YELPS**

Gillette ⤳ *n.*
Five-bladed Cutlass that promises a Man the Chin of Messrs Tiger **WOODS**, Roger **FEDERER** or Thierry **HENRY**, Son of Lenny

Gin ⤳ *n.*
pleasant Juniper Libation, Consumption of which does loosen the Tongue, the Tear-Duct, the Britches and, in Time, Civilisation

Mister Wm. **HOGARTH** *once averr'd that Gin does grease the Slope down which Society may slide unto Ruin. Yet*

HOGARTH *has not visited the Wine Lodge of Mister*
YATES, *for there he would see how fangl'd Physick-Bottles*
of Alcoholick-Pop do in fact perform this dread Role

Glastonbury ⇸ *n.*
Farmer's Field wherein **OAFS** enact the Battle of
Marston Moor accompany'd by Musick & **NARCOTICKS**

Gorillaz ⇸ *n.*
Mister **ALBARN'S** Troupe of illustrated **MINSTRELS**; a
mere Cartoon accompany'd by Musick & Doggerel

Granada ⇸ *n.*
in Spain, a Region of hot Climate & bronz'd Earth; in
England, a televis'd Region of hot Tempers & bronz'd
Women

Grand Prix ⇸ *n.*
Itinerant Travelling-Circus Chariot Race; watch'd by
Dullards, paid for by Watchmakers & **DISTILLERS**

Only a Dunder-Head could make Conversation 'pon the
dread Topick of Grand Prix, for it involves the base Error of
Attributing the Means of the Engineer 'pon the Character
of the Chariot-Driver. 'Sir, you say that Mister **HAMILTON**
is a Man of Parts, yet surely you mean that Meinherr
BENZ *is a Man of great Pistonry'*

Gravy ⇸ *n.*
noxious ELIXIR of curious Provenance, thought to be
the Works of myſtick culinary Deviant Miſter BISTO

Gritting ⇸ *ger.*
Winter Aĉtivity of which Mention is never made, except
by Reference to its not having taken PLACE

Guitar Hero ⇸ *n.*
Pantomime perform'd with a plaſtick LUTE; oft more
entertaining than an aĉtual Recital

G Is For Gambling

Gambling does arrange the many Vices of the
Englishman into one convenient Paſtime. Herein John
BULL can partake in his sentimental Love of Animals, his
drunk'n Bravado, his Ability to talk platitudinously 'pon
Matters Ṡporting & his Haplessness with Figures.

Gambling does unite the Passions of the Gentry & the
lower Orders. Both do revel in hard Cash, unruly Dogs &
reckless Wagering. However, both are so separat'd at the
Races & the Card Table that they have no Occasion to
combine & wage War 'gainſt the milque-toaſt Morals of
the pious middling Sort.

A man may sail two Routes into Gambling. The fleshy
Lighthouse that does guide Voyagers down the firſt
Route is Miſter John McCRIRICK, a harrumphing

Clotpoll of a Man, clad in such Whiskers & Tweed-Cloths as to resemble a hawkish Toby-Jug or an aristocratick Cousin of corpulent Jester Mister Royston **BROWN**. Fool **MCCRIRICK** does entice a Man to Gambling thro' unruly Manner & Gestickulation that some call Tic-Tac but which is more rightly term'd the Throwing of Shapes. The alternative Route is thro' the electronick Æther of th'Internet, whereby a Man may unburden himself of all Monies free of the shaming Gaze of his Fellows.

Those that run & those that do ride are enumerat'd below:

Ascot ⤳ *n.*
ritual Royal Jest at which their **MAJESTIES** deign to pass a Day in the Company of the Subject Sporting the most ridiculous **HAT**

Betting Shop ⤳ *n.*
Reliquary for the Storing of smash'd Hopes & brok'n Dreams, conveniently found in Neighbourhoods of the lower Orders

Cheltenham ⤳ *n.*
Town of Ireland, curiously situated in Gloucestershire; Inhabitants either thirsty or equine

Greyhound ⤳ *n.*
sinuous Hound condemn'd to pursue a Hare on Pain of Death or, worse, Affection from Cockneys

Horseracing → *n.*
the Wagering of Monies 'pon the Galloping of Steeds;
the Quest to impose order 'pon Nature thus imposes
chaos 'pon People

Jockey → *n.*
Satin-Clad Man deem'd sufficiently Small both to cling
on to a bolting Steed & to provoke no Alarm in Miss
Clare **BALDING**

Online Poker → *n.*
Card-Seance at which a Man can lose his Shirt afore the
World from the Convenience of his own Garret

Tipster → *n.*
Savant charg'd with foretelling how a Man shall lose his
Money

G Is For Green

The righteous Man does dedicate much of his Efforts in
this Life to preparing his earthly Estate in readiness for
Salvation in the **NEXT**. Today that Salvation is found in
Matters **GREEN**: the stewarding of the Earth that its
Bounteousness may not give out like a guttering Tallow-
Lamp or a once-proud Tin of Mister **ROWNTREE'S**
Quality Street now void save for **NOUGAT**.

Matters Green are often most vexatious. For a Man

must trade the Pleasures of Life now for the Security of Life in the far distant future in order to be Green; an Exchange that any who has observ'd ale-sodden Friday Brawls beyond Mister **YATES'** Wine Lodge will know Humanity is famously ill-suited to make.

If Individuals may not forego sufficient to preseve the Environment, then Hopes do rest with Climate Summits, a Parlour Game play'd in the Cities of Kyoto & Copenhagen, whereby Ambassadors ask their mighty Neighbours 'to place fewer Coals 'pon the Fire, oft in vain.

The Quest for Green does come with a great moral **INVERSION**. For much that was once regarded as an Object of Desire is now recast as an Object of Derision. We must forego such Conveniences as Mister **FORD'S** Capri-Chariot, the Merchant's Provision-Sack & all such Trinketry as is carv'd from the Forests of Java or the Pelt of th'Orang-utan should we wish to be sound Environmentally, & must forsake the antient English Custom of burning India-rubberis'd Tyres 'pon Feast-Days. A Thatch-Hair'd Bohemian who did once disregard the Merchant in his Swabian Cayenne Carriage with mere Envy may now do so with burning moral Superiority, all of which binds the laudable Sentiments of Greenery to the incens'd Odour of Priggery.

Conversely, many Barbarisms of the lowly Peasantry have acquir'd Halos of Respectability as now they are deem'd Green. The Eating of mud-cak'd local Produce &

the Deprivation of Infants with bare wooden Toys have somehow return'd to polite Society. He who picks over Life's Midden in Search of Scraps is no longer despis'd as a Ragman but hail'd as a Recycler. In this Inversion, all that is symbolick of the Green Cause is subjeckt to Veneration bordering on Idolatory. The Polar Bear is forgiv'n his Reign of Tyranny 'gainst Seals, Hudson Bay Fur Trappers & Mister **FOX'S** Glacier-Mints, for now he is a comely white-clad Standard Bearer for the Despoilation of Arctic Ice-Caps.

Those who do find the Natural Philosophy of Environmentalism to be incomplete or displeasing may simply choose otherwise. Fortuitously for them, a contrary Science is available, propos'd on behalf of the altruistick Funds of concern'd Oil-Merchants.

Herewith not'd Terms & Definitions of Green:

Area the Size of Wales ⇸ *n.*
Unit of Measurement for environmental Losses; most apt, as Wales is both of known Size & of fam'd Desolation

Bag for Life ⇸ *n.*
pious Sack so imposing that he who carries one is then oblig'd to house it for all **ETERNITY**

Carbon Footprint ⇸ *n.*
cant Term for the Sum of Fuel that an Individual does consume; morally less a Footprint than a **SHADOW** or **HALO**

Carbon Neutral ⇥ *n.*
much-desir'd State of Equilibrium at which one's
Righteousness does match one's Level of
Consumption

Climate Change Denier ⇥ *n.*
Heretick whose Fate is to be burn'd at the Stake of
publick Opinion or funded by Producers of **Oil**

Composting ⇥ *n.*
foul Decay of rotting Goods that would normally raise
Cries for Slum Clearance were it not practis'd by the
middling Sort

Food Miles ⇥ *n.*
moral Geography holding a Turnip from yonder Field
to be more pleasing than a Truffle from yonder
Piedmont

*Food Miles may yet be the most disputatious moral
Calculus since that perform'd by Mister* **Bentham.** *It
holds Distance to be the Measure of all that is righteous.
Thus a mighty Beefsteak husbanded with all the Bounty of
the Earth is superior to a meagre Bounty Bar transported
by a Ship 'pon the Sea. I myself do adhere unto Food Miles
by sending forth an Errand-Boy to near Billingsgate for all
Provisions, a simple & economickal Expedient that I would
commend unto* **All**

Global Warming ➻ *n.*
gradual Heating of the Atmosphere; felt strongly by
those who live 'pon Ice, question'd by those who live
'pon OIL

Hybrid ➻ *n.*
Whigs, when enlivened by Porto & Madeira, become
enthusiastick for Mister TOYOTA'S Japann'd Electronick-
Carriage

> *In Whiggish Boroughs such as Brighton & Hampstead, the
> greatest Peril 'pon the Highways is the threat of being
> struck by a wraithlike Prius, for it does creep forth 'pon the
> oblivious Pedestrian under a Cloak of electronick*
> SILENCE

Inconvenient Truth ➻ *n.*
Mister GORE'S Leckture on Climactick-Change; most
persuasive, save unto the CHINAMAN, who must forego
his Tallow-Oil

Low-Energy Bulb ➻ *n.*
wan electrick-Candle that creates the Effeckt, not so
much of Light, but of a SPECTRE in the Room

Recycling Bin ➻ *n.*
Wishing-Well in to which Persons do propel their Waste
in ardent Hope of Sanctifickation

Solar Panels ⤳ *n.*
Armour-Plate for the Roof, a Cladding that does imbue
a House with the very Power of **APOLLO**

Sustainable ⤳ *adj.*
that which may be done without Detriment unto the
Environment, such as preaching in a most righteous
Manner

Wind Farm ⤳ *n.*
mighty Pinwheel erect'd for the Purposes of generating
Power or the Annoyance of Mister Noel **EDMONDS**

> *A Wind Farm, beyond its praiseworthy Purpose of rousing
> Mister Noel* **EDMONDS'** *Ire, is a most potent Symbol of
> the Modern. Thus all the Pamphlets, Handbills &
> Literature of Nincompoops who crave Modernity come
> bedeck'd with Etchings of Windfarms. I would aver that if
> there is a Windfarm 'pon the Cover, there is a Poltroon
> behind it*

H *is for* HALLOWE'EN

Hallowe'en ⇾ *n.*
Holiday of the Deceas'd, adapted in the American
Manner with lesser Diabolism & greater Gluttony

Happy Meal ⇾ *n.*
box'd Supper from which an Infant may feaſt 'pon a
Figurine, Toy or Trinket &, on Occasion, 'pon broil'd
Meat

> *Hapless beef-barking Clown Miſter Ronald* **McDonald**
> *is oft flung into the Stocks for all the Ills that do befall*
> *Society, from the ballooning Arses of the lower Orders unto*
> *the Befouling of the Streets & the reckless Broiling of*
> *Apple-Paſtries unto the Heat of the* **Sun**. *In his Defence, I*
> *would aver that Miſter* **McDonald** *dresses no more*
> *comickally, nor wears his Skin paler, nor dines differently*
> *from his fellow Scotch-Men & that the Raising of the*
> *Temperature of Apples unto that of the solar* **Furnace** *is*
> *a scientifick Achievement worthy of Miſter* **Faraday**

Health & Safety ⇾ *n., adj.*
canting legaliſtick **Nanny**, forewarning a dumb cow-
like Publick that Coffee be **Hot** & that Nuts may
contain **Nuts**

Hello! ⇾ *n.*
gaudy Catalogue of the Lives of Ariſtocrats & Aċtresses;
its Piċtures do far outshine the banal Salt-Porridge of its
Writing

Hi-Def ⇢ *adj.*
Render'd in intricate Detail, so that wealthy Seekers of
Perfection may observe the pock-mark'd Visages of
Actors for Pleasure

High Five ⇢ *vb.*
to proffer a Hand-Slapp'd Affirmation, as if to ingratiate
oneself with either an Infant or a **SIMPLETON**

 A Man who does proffer the High Five is closer to the
 suck'd Thumb than to the shak'n Hand. Sir, I shall no
 sooner give you Ten than give you Ten glancing Blows
 with a Broad-Sword

Hooligan ⇢ *n.*
hot-blood'd Fool who brandishes Mister **STANLEY'S**
Knife & berates, 'Who art thou? Who art thou?'

 The Hooligan's Art is now solely preserv'd by the
 Nostalgia of corpulent Men in Middle-Age, who would
 hearken back unto an Epoch in which their younger Selves
 might propel a plastick Chair 'gainst a Bow Street Runner
 whilst clad in ornate Germanick Sporting-Slippers

Hotel ⇢ *n.*
Inn at which a Traveller may avail himself of such
Necessities as an electronick Britches-Press & a
Lilliputian Tea-Kettle

Gene HUNT → *n.*
red-carriag'd, reptile-shod Bow Street Runner; widely
held to be the very Incarnation of John **BULL** himself

H Is For Hair

'Tis a sorry Law of politickal Economy that when the
Populace has satisfy'd its moſt basick Needs, it will divert
its Expenditure towards **TRIFLES**. No sooner have the
common Populace conquer'd the Ills of Want &
Starvation than they do inveſt in the Grooming &
Teasing of their Hair.

Thus the true Purpose of Hair, namely to furnish
Lodging for divers Beetles, Ticks & Lice & to provide a
reſting-Place for a **PERIWIG**, is loſt unto Hiſtory.

Similarly, the ancient Profession of Barber-Surgeon
suffers a Decadence: Men once employ'd to extrackt
Teeth with Forceps & Gall-Stones with Pokers are
reduc'd to the low Station of Crimpers & Teasers, engag'd
in canting Discourse with those whose Locks they craft.
Thus:

'*Whither are you going on Holiday, Dr* **JOHNSON***?*'
'*Silence, Barber. A Gentleman brooks no Talk of his Feriation.*'
'*And a ribbon'd Sheath of Sheep's-Gut in the French Manner
for the Weekend . . . ?*'

And in the meaneſt of Boroughs are to be found more
Salons for the Dressing of Hair than Schools for the

Raising of Minds. Such Salons do solicit for Trade with the moſt egregious Word-Jouſts, viz. Curl Up & Dye; Thou Art Condemn'd To Dye; The Whig Intereſt; Jeremy **BENTHAM'S** Head-onism, &c.

For some, Hair does supplant Virtue as a Barometer of moral Standing, as if to befall the grievous Afflicktion of a Bad Hair Day does subjeckt a Person unto the Wrath of the **LORD**. 'Tis certain that those eminent Divines Messrs John & Chas. **WESLEY** did not adjudge the Route from Damnation unto Salvation by Hair Days Good & Bad.

Yet Hair does bring forth its own moral Judgement. As Time does work its Passage, Men do bald, all tend unto grey & all do see the Vainglory of those that scheme to cheat **FATE**. He who does dye & o'er-comb does not guise his Baldness but does advertise his Folly. Divers Cuts 'pon the Topick of Hair do follow:

Afro ⇸ *n.*
commendable Hair Halo, firſt ſport'd by Messrs Leo **SAYER** & Arthur **GARFUNKEL**, later adopt'd by Peoples of African Descent

Bouffant ⇸ *adj.*
puff'd with Air in a Style both ſtrutting & gaudy; a Term taken unsurprisingly from the **FRENCH**

Combover ⇸ *n.*
late Aᷗ of Vainglory whereby a Man brushes remaining Strands o'er a bald Head, as if to thatch a boil'd **EGG**

Conditioner ⇢ *n.*
scalp-unguent hastily rubb'd to ward off the dread
Effeckts of **SHAMPOO**

Extensions ⇢ *n.*
ghoulish Employ of the Locks of a Pauper 'pon a
Woman of Means: thus a cautionary Parable for the
Scalp

Goatee Beard ⇢ *n.*
uncheek'd Beard, said by Wearers to frame a rounded
Face & by observers to resemble a portly Daemon

Hairspray ⇢ *n.*
potent Miasma, one Breath of which does turn all Hair
in to **STONE**, most inexplickably describ'd as a naturall
Look

Hair Straighteners ⇢ *n.*
ceramick Torture-Irons us'd to extract a Woman's
Confession that she does wish to be Miss Cat **DEELEY**

Highlights ⇢ *n.*
sorrowful Streaks, intended to suggest a sunlit Aspect;
more oft to suggest a Strike from the Contents of a
Night-Soil-Bucket

Implant ⇢ *n.*
great Divots of Arse-Down, trepann'd in to the Skull for
Vanity: a Practice so barbarous that 'tis only endors'd by
Sports-Men

Mullet → *n.*
Centurion's Plume of Man-Hair worn neat at the
Crown & wild at the Neck; believ'd to be Germanick in
Origin

H Is For Hip-hop

Hip-Hop is oft defin'd as rhythmick Oratory set to a Beat;
heralded as the inventive Poetry of the Streets & then
condemn'd for all the Ills of Mankind.

A Man who does pracktise Hip-Hop is in equal Part a
Town-Crier, Poet, Peacock & Highway-Man.
Pracktitioners of Hip-Hop do include lisping
Numismatist Mister Fifty **CENT**, Mister Grand-Master
FLASH & his Quintet of **FURY** & double-barrell'd Canine
Mister Snoop **DOGGY DOGG**.

Such a Motley of Titles does indicate a most high
Self-Regard amongst the aristockracy of Hip-Hop.
Indeed, it is most certain that the aforesaid Rappers are
in keen Want of a Wife, or to secure Entry unto polite
Society, for they do boast most ardently of their
Prowess in the Bed-Chamber & their Reserves of
GOLD. The Poets of Hip-Hop do advertise their
esteem'd Status by riding in what they deem Pimp'd
Carriages, with Cart-Wheels gilded in Silver-Plate,
while they adorn themselves with such a Surfeit of
Gold, Diamonds, sundry Plate & **TREASURE** that they

might provoke a raid 'pon themselves from a Barbary Pirate or from the Spanish **NAVY**.

Those who would deny that there is an Art unto Hip-Hop & suppose that any Person can be proficient in Spoken Rhyme have never heard the abominable attempts of Mister John **BARNES** or Miss Debbie **HARRY**.

Thus if it is Art, it does merit Definition. A Rendering of Hip-Hop Lyricks does depict a most diverse Subjeckt-Matter, from Lust unto Violence & unto Lust. Consider:

'I favour the larger Fundament & I cannot **LIE**; nor can my esteem'd Brothers deny'

'I have nigh on one Hundred **PROBLEMS**, yet my **WENCH** is not one'

'My Milk-Cart brings all the Rakes unto the Yard forthwith, and verily, it is better than **THINE**'

'Do not call this a Come-Back, Sir, I have been here for Years. The late Mrs **JOHNSON** compels me to knock you **INSENSIBLE**'

''Tis like a Jungle out there, oft-times I wonder how I keep from going **UNDER**. Push me not, **SIR**, I am close 'pon the Edge. I try, most ardently, not to lose my **HEAD**'

A Journey unto the Highlands of Hip-Hop does take Mister Jas. **BOSWELL** *& myself to the South & Central of Los Angeles, in Alta California. The Brothers of the twin Parishes of* **INGLEWOOD & COMPTON** *are in my House. Compell'd to shout them* **OUT**. *Wrack'd by a sneezing Fit, I take a blue Kerchief from my left Pocket, thus enraging my Brethren in* **INGLEWOOD**. *Much afear'd: every Stage-Coach could be a Drive-By* **FUSILLADE**. *To paraphrase Mister* **CUBE**, *to-day was not a good Day*

I *is for* ITSU

Implants → *n.*
insincere Globules, worn athwart the Frontiſpiece of a
Strumpet

Innit → *contr.*
a Contracktion of is it not, said for Emphasis: *Admiral*
BYNG *was shot pour encourager les autres, innit*

Intelligent Design → *n.*
cant Philosophy supposing the World created by a
kindly Watchmaker: a more pleasing Lullaby than
th'actual **SCIENCE**

iPhone → *n.*
Miſter **JOBS'** Pocket-Trinket, which can perform all
domeſtick Tasks save ſteering a Stage-Coach or ridding a
Periwig of **BEETLES**

> *My favour'd iPhone Applickations are the Highway-Man
> Detector & the Exchange betwixt English **POUNDS** &
> Spanish **DUCATS***

Itsu → *n.*
Japann'd Tavern that dares serve Sushi. Fish serv'd Raw?
Am I a Sea-Gull, **SIR**?

The IVY → *n.*
hallow'd Hoſtelry where Peasants come to gape at celebrat'd Diners such as Messrs Julian **CLARY** & Chr. **BIGGINS**

I Is For Internet

Like a ne'er-ending Cheapside Coffee-House or an infinite Shelf of my Lord **HARLEY'S** Library, the Internet does bind all the Wits & all the Knowledge of the World in one almighty Highway of ÆTHER. This Super-Highway is as treacherous as any Turnpike, for it is laid with lewd Aquatints of Harlots & foreign Offers of Quack-Medicine. And, like any of the King's Highways, it does fall Prey to electronick Highway-Men, who might make like a Cut-Purse 'pon a Man's Banking-Deeds. Any Corner of the Internet whence Harlots do emerge to show a Flash of Stocking-Top are likely to be teeming with Footpads, who wait in Readiness to pilfer an unsuspeckting Gentleman's Pass-Words should he pass a Door mark'd **CLICK HERE**.

The free Passage of Information is said to be a Marvel of the Internet by all save those who do live by the Pen. Lowly Hacks & Minstrels such as Messrs Jas. **MURDOCH & METALLICA** do berate the Internet for taking the Bread from their indigent Mouths.

Opinion, which is Free in the Sense of without Cost or Value, does certainly move as swiftly 'pon the Internet as the Pox does move through a Bagnio. One Ignoramus may preach his Ignorance unto the whole World, while his Audience may respond in Kind. Such Debate does depart from the classickal Athenian Rules of Rhetorick, unfolding thus:

I say unto you that Mister **JENNER'S** *Vaccine does cause Enfeeblement & Dropsy. I counter, saying that the Govt. does hide the Whereabouts of mystickal flying Carriages from far Moons. I refute both, by comparing the'aforesaid Arguments unto the Credo of hateful Habsburg Corporal* **HITLER**.

An ever-eddying Current of Information added unto a ready Supply of Dunces does make good Hunting-Ground for a Hot-Head seeking to press-gang a **MOB**. Any Man who does add his Name unto a Petition or forward a Missive unto his Friends does raise an electronick Pitch-Fork & can be led to march on any Foe, from a Merchant-Adventurer who does pollute the Seas with Oil to an impertinent Wretch who does not show sufficient Respeckt unto Mister Stephen **FRY**. The Mob of th'Internet does swing both Tory & Radical, ready to lay Siege in equal Numbers 'gainst those who warn of the warming Globe & those who would deny it.

Perhaps the greatest Conflation of Information & Folly is to be found in th'ethereal Marketplace call'd eBay. Those who **USE** eBay do marvel that one may unearth the rarest of Heirlooms from the entire Treasure-Chest of Humanity. Yet those who **OBSERVE** eBay do marvel how one may find the rarest of Fools who would veritably part with Money for the worthless Jetsam in Mankind's Attic. He who bids at Auction for a Plethora of Etch'd **CARDS** from a long-defunct Tobacco-Manufacturer is not a noble Hunter for Treasure but a **CLOT**.

Those who make Community 'pon the Internet have

develop'd their own demotick, a barbarous Cant of Abbreviations. Herein one may salute a Fellow's Wit by averring **LOL** in Stead of 'I Do Laugh Out Loud, In The Manner Of **FALSTAFF**' or **ROFL** in rightfull Place of 'I Do Roll 'Pon The Floorboards As Might A Bedlamite Hysterick'. To them, I say **RTGD**: *Read The Godforsak'n Dictionary!*

Herewith the Terms most search'd for:

Amazon ⇥ *n.*
electronick Clairvoyant who claims to foretell a Man's every Taste & Manners from his earlier Perusal of Books

Face-Book ⇥ *n.*
Almanack wherein People do catalogue their Achievements for publick Consumption; thus a strutting Compendium of **PEACOCKERY**

Google Street View ⇥ *n.*
cartographick Espionage whereby one peers into the Homes of Strangers on Pretence of consulting the Map

Instant Messenger ⇥ *n.*
Task of Communication properly perform'd by a Messenger-Boy; today delegat'd to Mister Wm. **GATES**

iPlayer ⇥ *n.*
Ingenious Reprise of last night's Electrickal-Theatre presentations, from sainted Mister **DIMBLEBY** to Man-Suet Master **CORDEN**

LinkedIn ⇸ *n.*
a ghoſtly Coffee-House of Commerce in which the
recently unemploy'd do remind the working World of
their **EXISTENCE**

MySpace ⇸ *n.*
barren electronick Tundra haunted by loſt Souls in
Search of whiter Teeth or unsign'd **MINSTREL-ACTS**

Skype ⇸ *n.*
great Looking-Glass into which a man may Stare &
converse with a slow-moving Shadow of his **FELLOW**

Viral ⇸ *n.*
transient Marvel that passes thro' the Internet, viz. a Cat
proficient at the Forte-Piano; an Infant who **MAY** or
MAY NOT talk

YouTube ⇸ *n.*
electronick Gallery moſt easily tour'd in order to see
exhibits of all the World's **STUPIDITY**

J *is for* JUST FOR MEN

J. Lo ⇢ *n.*
Singer & Actress descended from the Block: both her
Name & her Talent are abbreviated, most unlike her
Hind-Quarters

Jacuzzi ⇢ *n.*
turbulent Bath-Tub with an in-built **FLATULENCE**
rendering unnecessary that of its Occupant

Jenga ⇢ *n.*
intricate Game of Construction that demonstrates both
a Wood-Block's Property of Friction & a Person's
Tolerance of Futility

Jersey ⇢ *n.*
fabl'd Island-Kingdom for Men who evade the Excise;
viz. Mister Charles **HUNGERFORD** & his lone Protector,
Mister James **BERGERAC**

Jigsaw ⇢ *n.*
pointless Mutilation of well-lov'd Art proffer'd to the
elderly Publick for laborious Reconstruction

JOHN LEWIS ⇢ *n.*
Mercers where the middling Sort of people do pay to
QUEUE with those of like Mind

> *The middling Sort, while fearing the Rise of the working*
> *Masses in all other Aspeckts of Life, do swoon in Praise at*
> *the Community of Diggers & Levellers of which the* **JOHN**

LEWIS *Partnership is compris'd, as if an Antimacassar bought from one is somehow bless'd with superior Virtue*

Jordan ⇥ *n.*
promiscuous Termagant who does cavort, marry & raise Infants at the Mercy of the publick Gaze

The life of Miss **JORDAN** *is so publick that she does solicit for Suitors 'pon the electronick Bear-Pit of reality Television. Tho' why a Woman should forsake her christen'd Name of Miss Katie* **PRICE** *for the Mantle of the Hashemite Kingdom of* **TRANSJORDAN** *is unknown unto Mankind*

Jungle ⇥ *n.*
antipodean Forest us'd by England as a penal colony for Bedlamies & pendulous Mummers; out of which a Celebrity may be **GOT**

Just For Men ⇥ *n.*
fantastickal Mercury-Powder that both shades once-grey Hair & restores a Man's lost Libido, Youth, Parts, &c.

Fully Half of the World's Supplies of th'aforesaid Elixir have been spent to glaze the Tonsure of Mister Tom **JONES,** *thus rendering his Scalp a Monopoly Supplier*

K *is for* KRANKIE

Karaoke ↝ *n.*
Japann'd Art of encasing the most infernal Song in a confin'd **ROOM**

> *The Japann'd Art of Karaoke does defy the Lexicographer's Craft, for it does entail a Word not pronounc'd as it is* **SPELT,** *a Song not sung as its Composer* **INTENDED** *& a Performance by a dreadful Braggart more in his Cups than he* **REALIS'D**

Katona ↝ *adj.*
simultaneously to be beset by all possible Travails of moral Life

> *Thus one Soul, burden'd by great Avoirdupois, Miasmas of Cockaigne-Powder, fiendish Debt & froz'n Foodstuffs before Noon-time, may be said to be* **KATONA'D**

Kentucky Fried Chicken ↝ *n.*
Spic'd Poultry of th'Americkan Militia, thought to contain Capsicum, Saltpetre, Mercury & **SULPHUR**

Killer ↝ *adj.*
that which is most laud'd or esteem'd, a Term thus rarely applied unto actual People who kill

The Killers ↝ *n.*
unkempt Hymners of theological Contradiction, viz. 'I have Soul, but I am not one of his Majesty's Red-Coats'

Kraftwerk ⇸ *n.*
Teutonic clockwork Automaton-Choriſters who profess
Admiration for Dressmakers' Mannequins, Turnpikes &
the grand Tour of FRANCE

Krankies ⇸ *n. pl.*
base Inversion of godly Family Law whereby a Man
makes a Son of his Wife & suffers divers
IMPERTINENCES from Him or Her

Kwik-Fit ⇸ *n.*
Troupe of Tumbler-Mechanicks whom one cannot
BETTER, eſp. in the twin Endeavours of Cart-Wheels &
Truſt

L *is for* LAPDANCING

Lager → *n.*
efficacious Swipe belov'd of Antipodean **CONVICTS**, damn'd **COLONIALS**, pox'd **CONTINENTALS** & divers ſporting **HOOLIGANS**

Lapdancing → *n., vb.*
a Cinderella Cousin to Harlotry, for it is perform'd in glass Slippers

Las Vegas → *n.*
Brothel & Gaming Den, seemingly own'd by Cut-Purses, hoſted by Miſter Billy **BUTLIN** & polic'd by Messrs **BURKE & HARE**

Latte → *n.*
warm'd Milk-Drink, partaken by Media Man-Children & publicity **HARLOTS** to delay the Onset of Bed-Time

Lego → *n.*
Norsemen's **CONSPIRACY** of fiendish plaſtickated Brick-work design'd to keep England's Infants in **SERVITUDE**

Legoland → *n.*
Harlequin Brick Kingdom govern'd on the false Principle that something render'd smaller may somehow furnish greater Enjoyment

Licence Fee → *n.*
mild Excise, loudly suppos'd to fund Licentiousness, while quietly bringing News & Erudition unto the Nation

Like ⇸ *conj.*
a barbarous cant Term meaning juſt as, or charact-
erising report'd Speech

> *His Maj. King* **GEORGE III** *is like, 'By G-d, England shall
> have Satisfaction 'gainſt the French,' & General* **WOLFE** *is
> like, 'I shall beſt them at the Siege of Quebec.' Hiſtory does
> record that England did, like, totally vanquish the French
> & His Maj. King Louis XV got serv'd*

Literary Feſtival ⇸ *n.*
genteel Summit where Authors suffer the middling
Sort to queſtion them on Condition of buying their
Works in Droves

LOLcat ⇸ *n.*
Folk-Art wherein feline Thoughts are
ANTHROPOMORPHIS'D & Principles of Grammar
VIOLAT'D for the Amusement of the Masses

LP ⇸ *n.*
Shellac Discs, engrav'd with Patterns of Delight or
Incomprehension, according to the Age of the Beholder

L Is For London

Dullards oft entreat me to repeat my Aphorism that
when a Man is tir'd of London, he is tir'd of Life. This I do,

with the weary Countenance of an antient Sports-man, press'd in to Service as an after-Dinner Raconteur. Permit me some Clarifickation: there is much of Life in London, most of it **Tiresome**.

For the Metropolis is Home to some seven Million Souls, each striving to ignore his Fellows.

And London is said to be an Accretion of Villages & thus an equal Accretion of **Village-idiots**. Each Parish or Hundred is bless'd with a Character of its own, oft so attractive unto the money'd Resident that they do congregate in the Area & thus drive out the Character. Mister Richard **Curtis** does portray Notting Hill as a quaint Village of Book-Binders & Bohemians with such Compulsion that no Book-Binder or Bohemian may hope to live there.

London is oft celebrat'd as a City of great Diversity, that is to say the wealthy Man does live next to the meanest Artisan, & a Person's Neighbour may be of any Creed or Nation. Thus a Londoner may delude himself to be as cosmopolitan as **Erasmus** if he does so much as buy a Barrel of Hummus Bean-Paste, heed a Gaggle of Street-Minstrels who serenade him with Pipes of Pan, or hail a Carriage driv'n by a Fellow from the Gold Coast. *Bravo, Mister Resident of* **London***, for you have stood in Line next to a Dutchman & an Americkan Colonial. Do you expect to receive a* **Biscuit** *for yr. Achievements?*

So great is the Variety of the City that the Resident of London is oblig'd to buy the **Time Out** periodickal

merely to remain abreast of the divers Performances &
Festivals that he shall later not attend.

Herewith a Guide unto the great City:

O2 Centre ↠ *n.*
Spectral Tent, pitch'd without the Borders of London so
that diabolickal Showmen may seek Refuge under it

Acton ↠ *n.*
Destination for those once deport'd unto penal
Colonies; each Tenement stack'd with one score of
Barkeeps from Van Diemen's Land

Camden ↠ *n.*
Market teeming with rain-sodd'n **EMO** Youths whose
lackadaisical Road-Crossing does obstruckt the smooth
Passage of my Sedan-Chair

Covent Garden ↠ *n.*
most forlorn Piazza, for here Tourists do come to
Glimpse the true London yet see merely other Tourists

*A Tourist who pays a Visit unto Covent Garden in Search
of the true Capital would surmise that the People of the
City go clad in gaily-colour'd Rain-Coats, do travel in great
huddl'd Packs & do refer to each other as Mon Cher*
PIERRE, PAOLO, & GUNTHER

Docklands Light Railway ↬ *n.*
phantom Transportation whereby Carriages without
Drivers glide betwixt Offices without People

Fleet Street ↬ *n.*
now bereft of Scriveners & Presses, a Highway giv'n
over to Messrs **GOLDMAN & SACHS** and the Mercers of
TIE-RACK

Hampstead ↬ *n.*
worthy Hill-Village, said to provide Shelter unto an
elusive Band of liberal Minds & their pious Opinions

Harrods ↬ *n.*
greatest, most ornate Merchant-Hall in all the World:
here one sees everything save actual London-folk

> *The Origins of Harrods are shroud'd in Time: 'tis thought
> that here once stood a Shrine to the fallen Princess* **DIANA**,
> *around which grew a Series of Merchant-Stalls*

Knightsbridge ↬ *n.*
once Home to fashionable Londoners, now fortify'd for
Muscovite Mercenaries

London Eye ↬ *n.*
prophetick Ferris-Wheel, built to prove that London
does appear the more beautiful the further that you rise
away from it

Marylebone High Street ⇸ *n.*
much favour'd Thoroughfare, erect'd in Tribute to the
Patron-Saint of the plutocratick **COSTERMONGER**

> *At* **MARY-LE-BONE,** *the crown'd Heads of Europe do
> exchange Ingots of* **GOLD** *for Truckles of Cheese of similar*
> **VALUE.** *'Five & Thirty Guineas for a bag of Mushrooms?'
> 'Yes, Sir, for they have been bless'd by Saint* **MARY-LE-
> BONE** *& her High-Street.' Similar is to be found at Porto-
> Bello Market, where the money'd Interest do come to gape
> at weathered Vegetables & Broken* **FURNITURE**

Notting Hill Carnival ⇸ *n.*
Festival of Proportion: One Hundred arrested, one
Thousand clad as silver'd Butterflies, one Million
intoxicated

Shepherd's Bush ⇸ *n.*
most industrious of Boroughs, for 'tis Home to
th'almighty Iron-Smelting, Rag-Rendering Combine of
Mister **STEPTOE** & his **SON**

Tate Modern ⇸ *n.*
a derelict riverside Bedlam, since abandon'd by its
Inmates, now housing their distracted Daubs &
Sculptures

Madame TUSSAUDS ⇸ *n.*
futile Pilgrimage Site to which millions of Foreigners do
come each year to venerate wax'n half-Likenesses

132

Wembley ⇢ *n.*
Arena beſtrode by a vaſt Arch, so that all may have
Sight of the Place of England's ſporting Tribulations

Weſtminſter ⇢ *n.*
Parish of Govt. that, deſpite Barricades, foreboding
Portcullises & arm'd Guards, Politickians ſtill enter each
Day

M *is for* MIRACLE

Man-Boobs ⇢ *n. pl.*
gynaecomaſtial Malady that swells Man unto Woman's
wretch'd Eſtate: a Hazard of Gluttony

Marathon ⇢ *n.*
Aɕtivity at which Englishmen only excel when it does
refer to an Evening of adjacent televis'd EPISODES

Mario Bros ⇢ *n. pl.*
Genoese DUNNYKIN-MEN woefully ill-caſt in a
Struggle 'gainſt King BOWSER, myſteriously describ'd as
Super

Meerkat ⇢ *n.*
inseɕtivorous Afric Rodent now of greateſt Reknown
for the Sale of ASSURANCES for Curricles & Carriages

Mercury ⇢ *n.*
its Viɕtims including M-People, Gomez & Miss Speech
DEBELLE, Mercury is more deadly as a Musick Prize
than as a Poison

Microwave ⇢ *n.*
infernal Cupboard that can raise a Fruit-Pie unto the
Temperature of a Blacksmith's FORGE

Middle of the Road ⇢ *adj.*
favouring the Centre over hot-head Extremes: in
Politicks, an admirable Quality; in Musick, a deathly one

MILF ↣ *n.*
cant Term for a Woman in possession of a Child who does excite in Men the Urge to produce another

Minidisc ↣ *n.*
appall'd at the Simplicity of popular Musick, Mister **SONY**'s noble Endeavour to complickate it

Miracle ↣ *n.*
whereby the Face of our **SAVIOUR** is reveal'd in Sandwiches, cut Vegetables, &c.; more Proof of Credulousness than of Divinity

Modern Parenting ↣ *n.*
Scheme in which a Child is curs'd to Sport his Mother's Hair 'pon his Head & his Father's **OPINIONS** 'pon his Shirt

Mojito ↣ *n.*
a leaf-block'd Gutter of a Drink

Moleskine ↣ *n.*
Alchemick Note-Book that does render the inane Scribbling of its Owner in to purest **GOLD**

Mother ↣ *n.*
one who does birth & nurture Infants; now subjeckt of ribald Insults about suppos'd Fatness:

'Your mother is so beset with Corpulence that I was oblig'd to take a Coach-and-Four to reach her good Side.' 'No, Sir, I

aver that your Mother is so egregiously Fat that, should she receive a Cutlass-Blow, she would bleed **GRAVY**'

MP3 ⇸ *n.*
Musick compress'd in to ethereal Form to be of greater Convenience for Storage, Transportation & Theft

Musical ⇸ *n.*
The most slow-witt'd Branch of Stagecraft; its bovine Audience brought up from the Regions by **COACH**

> *To-day the Term Musical applies less to a Comick-Opera or diverting Charivari than to a worthless Patchwork of the collected Doggerel of Mister Rodney* **STEWART** *or Signor Francis* **VALLI** *& his Quarto of Seasons*

Music Journalism ⇸ *n.*
Binary Scrivening, either condemning the entire Historie or proclaiming a new **MESSIAH** of popular Musick each Week

M Is For Marriage

Modern Life is a ne'er-ending Quest to accrue Liberty & Money. Modern Marriage is a salutary Lesson in the grave Consequence of a Surfeit of Liberty & Money when apply'd unto the antient Custom of **MATRIMONY**.

For to-day, a Marriage is a Display less of matrimonial

Affecktion & ecclesiastical Rite than of free-spent CASH & the free Exercise of WHIMS.

Freedom is exercis'd 'pon the solemn Liturgy of Marriage. To-day, 'tis Custom for Bride & Groom to seleckt the Readings & craft the VOWS. Thus the Sermon of the Priest must compete 'gainst the mystick Colourings of Senor Paulo COELHO or 'gainst the whimsickal History of ursine Drudge Mister Winston the POOH & his needful porcine Catamite Master PIGLET. The solemn Vows that should rightly BIND & ENSLAVE the Couple in eternal Contrackt are now diluted unto a vague Agreement that each shall maintain a civil Tongue unto the Other until someone deem'd MORE FIT shall pass by.

The most fearsome words utter'd in Matrimony are not 'I do' but 'I wish to be treated like a Princess'. Seemingly the perfect Day is a Melding of despotick Power & the liberal Applickation of GLITTER. Thus Invitations are bedeck'd with sparkling Flim-Flam, as if deliver'd by the Faeries of the Woods & not by the Jenever-Soaks of the Penny-Post. The Bride's-Maids are truss'd in gaudy Frocks of deep fuschia & burgundy in order to resemble boil'd HAMS & thus not detrackt from the suppos'd Radiance of the Bride. To surmise, the Bride who wishes others to entreat her as a Princess shall find that most would eventually dispatch her in the Manner of sometime Princess MARIE ANTOINETTE.

Fully one in two Marriages do end in the Divorce

Courts. A reasonable Society should send forth fully one in two Weddings unto the **CRIMINAL** Courts. Herewith Aphorism & Definition for the divers Customs of Marriage:

Anniversary ⇸ *n.*
demarcating the Years since Matrimony, first mark'd by Dinner, then by Gifts & finally by an annual Act of Congress

Best Man ⇸ *n.*
honorifick that proclaims a Man proficient in Rhetorick, Logistick, Courtly Dancing & Diplomacy, & then proves him **INCAPABLE**

Civil Partnership ⇸ *n.*
Law extending the legal Benefit of Marriage unto Molly-Couples:

> *A most unusual Choice of Rights, for the effete Man has for many Years wisely enjoy'd the ornate Dressing & feverish Dancing associat'd with Weddings, while eschewing the forc'd Monogamy of legal Marriage*

Engagement Ring ⇸ *n.*
bejewell'd Wager that a Man shall remain faithful at a Price of two Months' Salary & one Diamond

First Dance ⇸ *n.*
Mating-Ritual dreaded by Dancers & Audience alike: it

does meld th'English Staples of Lust, Ceremony &
EMBARRASSMENT

Unschool'd in courtly Etiquette, the Englishman must be well-season'd before stepping 'pon the Dancing-Floor; for to tread there in a Condition of Sobriety would augur certain **DEATH**

Guests ⤳ *n.*
a Number of closest Relations & dearest Friends, divided by the Cost of Champagne

Hen Night ⤳ *n.*
Termagants' **COVEN** so fearsome that it must increasingly be conducted **ABROAD**

Honeymoon ⤳ *n.*
gilded Exile of Bride & Groom, who oft desire to be abandon'd in the Manner of Mister **CRUSOE**, *sans* Shoes, News & **CIVILISATION**

Morning Suit ⤳ *n.*
hir'd Raiments that oblige a Man to spend the most auspicious Day of his Life bedeck'd as his Majesty's **UNDER-BUTLER**

Pre-Nup ⤳ *n.*
priggish Gambit for those who would wager that their Capital shall outlive their Affecktion

Seating Plan ↝ *n.*
Arrangement of Chairs necessitating the diplomatick
Arts in Planning & Statecraft to mend th'inevitable
Border DISPUTES

Stag Party ↝ *n.*
A Day of Error where a Man pretends to be VIRILE a
Month before pretending to be CHASTE

Wedding Breakfaſt ↝ *n.*
pinch-fac'd English Banquet; Viands chosen not for
Deliciousness but for Ease of SLICING

Wedding Cake ↝ *n.*
vaſt Edifice of Marchpane, Raisins, &c., nicely cut &
diſtributed so that others may DISPOSE of it

Wedding Disco ↝ *n.*
Pagan Ritual to bind Newly-Weds thro' the diverting
MUSICK of Miſter RITCHIE'S All Night Long

> *English Common Law does ſtate that a Marriage is not
> valid until & unless the Congregation have danc'd the
> following Jigs: the All-Night-Long, the Come-On-Eileen, the
> Sweet Caroline, Miſter* JACKSON'S *Paternity Ballad of
> Billie-Jean & Miſter* SINATRA'S *Italianate Bombaſt New
> Amſterdam, New Amſterdam*

Wedding Liſt ↝ *n.*
Ransom Note that does set the Price on Friendship at
one Sauce-Pan, two Down-Pillows or six Glasses

M Is For Medicine

Nothing characterises the noble Progress of Man better than his Struggle 'gainst Disease.

For much of History, Man was condemn'd to succumb unto the most trifling of Agues for which Physick is today available. Inflam'd duelling Scars might today be salv'd by a Tincture of TCP, whilst Berocca is naught but a Physick-Cure for dread'd SCURVY.

Now eminent Barber-Surgeons, such as the many-titl'd Panjandrum Professor Doctor Lord Robert WINSTON & Mister BOOTS' inescapable Apotheckary, enable Man to conquer the most grievous of Ailments.

Yet Man is a Creature of VARIETY and thus, bor'd of proven Science, does conjour romantick Quackery to tend to his Imagination as much as his ILLS. Tiredness & Bloating do escalate from Man's naturall Estate unto the Status of treatable Symptoms that demand a ferment'd Milk-Cure.

He also yelps at the Prospeckt of the meanest Cough amassing the Velocity & Momentum of a dread'd EPIDEMICK. Nothing does augur greater Malady than an Englishman who says unto his Physician, 'I am fine.' To-day an Apotheckary's Handbill does counsel me to wash my Periwigs with a Tincture of Tar & hang my Windows with MERCURY-PAPER in Precaution 'gainst the SWINISH-FLU.

Herewith the great Varieties of Physick of the DAY:

Acupuncture ⇸ *n.*
the ſtabbing Treatment that can cure any Ill save
GULLIBILITY or the Fear of NEEDLES

Aromatherapy ⇸ *n.*
fanciful Cross-Breed of Medicine & Perfumery, where
Scent is presum'd to reſtore SIGHT; loſt LIMBS, &c

Chiropratic ⇸ *n.*
treatment to set a Patient's Bones by Hand & to crush a
Critick's Bones by LAWSUIT

> *I shall pass no Remark 'pon Chiropraſty save ──── ─ ────*
> *── ────.*

Homeopathy ⇸ *n.*
medicine of Proportion where smaller Dose is greater
Cure; a theory of which the more I read the less I
BELIEVE

Hot Stone Therapy ⇸ *n.*
practised in Persia, a barbarick Method of EXECUTION;
practised in an English Spa, a Method of RELAXATION

Reiki ⇸ *n.*
A Practice whereby Manual Manipulation of Energie
Force does relieve a Patient's PURSE if not his DISEASE

M Is For Money

The simple Man sees Money as a mere Medium of Exchange; Baubles that do permit one Man to purchase one of Miſter **GINSTER'S** Paſties without having to proffer an Hour of his Labour or a Bushel of Grain in Return. Such Simpletons are oft call'd **ECONOMISTS**: able to count the Value of a Transaction, yet blinded unto its Meaning.

For Money is more than the Form of Exchange: it is the Measure of Man's Standing amongſt his Fellows, the Objeckt of his Luſt & the Pass-Port that eases his Passage from the humbleſt Station in Life to the higheſt. Indeed, should a Man rise from the Peasantry unto a gild'd Bungalow in fair Essex or Cheshire, carry'd in Miſter **JAGUAR'S** Oaf-Carriage, it shall be through **MONEY**.

Likewise, Men of Learning & Intellect do affeckt to be unconcern'd with the vulgar Trappings of Money by maintaining a searing Contempt for all who have Money. The Poor do Deſþise the Rich while seeking to become them through Scratch-Cards, gaudy Visitations unto Caſtilian Spain & the simple Means of **THEFT**.

Money does allow the shrewd Observer to measure the To & Fro, the Ebb & Flow, but principally the Rise & Fall, of his Fellows. Herewith the Measures whereby Men do proffer, flaunt & inevitably lose th'aforesaid **MONEY**:

American Express → *n.*
invisible Cabal of Payment & Exchange; of such
Exclusivity that it is accept'd almoſt **NOWHERE**

Barclaycard → *n.*
plaſtick Cash once endors'd by Messrs Alan **WHICKER**
& Rowan **ATKINSON**, for Actors are true Paragons of
financial Husbandry

Cash Point → *n.*
a Teller's **NOOK**, conceal'd in ſtout Walls to secure Men's
CASH & to furnish Beggars with a Seat

Credit Card → *n.*
miraculous Rhombus of precious Plaſtick that, tho'
small, does conceal a vaſt Acreage of **DEBT**

> *The plaſtick Card has innumerable modern Uses, from the*
> *Facilitation of unaffordable Purchases, to th'Accrual of*
> *abſtrackt Miles to reward Loyalty unto Miſter* **BOEING'S**
> *Air-Carriage to Abandonment behind the Bar of a Tavern*
> *& e'en Cleaving Lines of the Cockaigne-Powder: all of*
> *them* **IMBECILICK**

Euro → *n.*
continental Currency that oft induces Apoplexy in
Englishmen; can also trade for meagre Coffee, thimbles
of Beer & bubbl'd Water

House Price ⇸ *n.*
in moſt Lands, a Trifle of Household Budgets; in England, the sole Measure of national **WEALTH &** personal **STANDING**

Mortgage ⇸ *n.*
Loan-Contraĉt whereby a Man gains his Home for a mere three hundred goug'd Payments & five and twenty Years of **ANGUISH**

Pension ⇸ *n.*
a Fool's Wager with Deſtiny: should I neither **DIE** nor make poor Choices, nor suffer the Excise-man, I shall be **RICH**

Pound Coin ⇸ *n.*
the basick Unit of Cash in Britain; moſt conveniently it can be exchang'd for an Item of no Worth in a Pound-Land

Scratch-card ⇸ *n.*
a Peasant's Token, promising a reſpite from Drudgery above its silvery Filigree, yet revealing Disappointment underneath

> *The National Lottery is oft criticis'd as a Tax 'pon the*
> *Ignorant, who are oblivious to the Odds of Viĉtory being*
> *scanter than the Odds that one may be ſtrick'n by*
> *Lightning & discover'd by Miſter Simon* **COWELL** *'pon the*
> *selfsame* **DAY.**

M Is For Motoring

Perhaps the greatest Lie of our Age is: 'My Carriage serves no Purpose save to transport me from Alpha unto Beta.' For beyond the winking red & orange Lanterns mount'd athwart it, the entire Carriage may be call'd an Indicator – of Status, of Rank & of Meaning.

For Dullards do make Judgements 'pon their Fellows according to their Choice of Carriage. He who chooses a People-Carrying Carriage does advertise his Fertility, or that he does labour for Messrs **ADDISON & LEE**. He who chooses a blacken'd Range Rover does proclaim himself a Merchant of Laudanum or a Wife of a Footballer. Conversely he who begins social Intercourse with the Question: 'What, Sir, do you drive?' merits no Riposte save: 'A Coach & Four through any Argument that you dare propose, Sir.'

The wretched Men who do choose a gaudy Carriage to aid their Courtship of Women do instead merely attrackt other Men, for a Conveyance is to Nincompoops as a Candle-Flame is to Moths. No Woman has ever beheld an Edition of varnish'd Oaf-Bible *What Car?* save in **PITY**. Observing the unquiet Mob that does comprise the Audience of Mister **CLARKSON'S** *Top Gear*, it is apparent that the few Females therein are held Captive in the Manner of Anglo-Saxon Women seiz'd by marauding Norsemen in **LONG-BOATS**.

Herewith a Purview of the Forecourt:

4X4 → *n.*
a Royal War of Succession in Carriag'd Form, prosecuted to proteckt the Children **WITHIN** by endangering Children **WITHOUT**

Audi → *n.*
Germanick Tinsmith whose silver'd Carriages provoke priapick Excitement amongst Architects, Draughts-Men & Media **BUFFOONS**

Convertible → *n.*
perverse Exchange that holds a Carriage Roof made of Broad-Cloth to be of greater Value than one made of Steel

Driving Test → *n.*
legal Examination declaring a Youth of seventeen Years approv'd to crash his Father's Carriage forthwith

Estate Car → *n.*
Carriage with a Back enlarg'd to convey Sporting Goods, pedigree Dogs & the Message that its Driver is of the middling Class

Ferrari → *n.*
Italianate Sporting-Curricle: it carries its Engine in its Rear, just as its Driver carries his good Sense

G-Wiz → *n.*
Signor **VOLTA**'s amusing transportational Toy that one Day may be us'd to carry actual Humans

HUMMER ⇸ *n.*
a colonial Fortress for the domestick Road; rais'd and
armour'd to shield the Rider from the Opprobrium of
those outside

Mini ⇸ *n.*
rotund Carriage, celebrat'd by Mister **CAINE** thro' the
Highways of Piedmont & debas'd by Mister **FOXTON**
thro' the Highways of London

Minicab ⇸ *n.*
Act of Brotherhood, where a Man may convey his
fellow great Distances without speaking one Word of
his Language

MOT ⇸ *n.*
Viva Voce to which a Carriage submits at three Years in
order to justify both its Safety and the Mechanick's
colossal Fee

Petrol-Head ⇸ *n.*
a Man most enamour'd of Motor Carriages. After
Conversation, it may be correckt to substitute the first
Word for **BLOCK**

Road Rage ⇸ *n.*
impotent Bravado provok'd by the Carriages of Others
yet project'd from the safety of a Carriage of one's own

Smart Car → *n.*
Carriage so tiny that it does appear as a wheel'd Cage for
a **GIANT**

>*Should Dean* **SWIFT** *have writt'n for our Age, he would
have imprison'd Mister Lemuel* **GULLIVER** *not under a
Bind of Ropes but captive behind the Wheel of a Smart Car*

Traffic → *n.*
Highway-blocking Midden of Rubber & Iron, strangely
blam'd on Others by those who do cause it

N *is for* NURSING HOME

Nacho ⇢ *n.*
triangulat'd Spanish Biscuit, flavour'd as a Footman's
SHOE

National Health Service ⇢ *n.*
To an Englishman, a seckular Religion; to an American,
a Leveller **ABOMINATION**

National Insurance ⇢ *n.*
a Shilling-Excise levied 'pon the Incomes of working
Folk; curiously it is not to be referr'd to as an Income
Tax

New Year Resolution ⇢ *n.*
Act of Deception: writt'n in December, enact'd in
January, discard'd in February & forgott'n in March

Night Bus ⇢ *n.*
Mister **BENTHAM'S** Panopticon 'pon Wheels: it does
trawl the Streets to impound nocturnal Ne'er-do-wells &
Vagrants

Non-Domiciled ⇢ *adj.*
preferring the Civilisation of England, but not the
Exchequer that does pay for it

Nostalgia ⇢ *n.*
backward Affecktion that Men are willing to **FEEL**, yet
not prepar'd to **PAY** for, viz. Woolworths, Shellac'd
musickal Recordings

Nursing Home ↛ *n.*
boil'd Cabbage Mausoleum in which sedat'd Senescents
may practise for very Death

Nutritionist ↛ *n.*
Practitioner of the charlatan-Science of Diet; most
prominent of whom is a Scotch Hedge-Witch, nam'd
Miss Gillian MᴄKᴇɪᴛʜ

N Is For Newsagents

The learn'd Man should not be without divers News-
Papers to enliven his Mind or to burden his Coffee Table.

The groaning Shelves of any Newsagent do attest that
there is a Title for every Faction of Opinion or Depth of
Pocket, whilst a furtive Glance skyward further attests
that there is a Publickation suit'd unto every lustful
Pecadillo.

Most confusingly the English do parse their Journals
& Handbills by the Nature of the Paper, viz. Tabloid,
Broad Sheet, Glossy, as if the learn'd Man should select
his reading Matter by Tᴏᴜᴄʜ.

'Pon the Sabbath the Custom is to print News-Papers
as countless component Folios in the Manner of Mister
Wm. Sʜᴀᴋᴇsᴘᴇᴀʀᴇ, at least if the Bard had writt'n
dunciad Screeds 'pon Style & Travel and not of Romeo &
Juliet.

Noblest of all in the Pursuit of print'd Matter is the Newsagent, the excellent Hindoo, Mussulman or Parsee who does rise afore Dawn to provision his Neighbours with urgent News, nourishing Tinctures of Lucozade or a score of Messrs **BENSON & HEDGES'** gild'd Tobaccory.

His Deliveries do include the following:

Beano ⇸ *n.*
esteem'd Journal pertaining to Matters menacing or gnashing & to the Pedagogy of **BASH STREET**

Daily Mail ⇸ *q.v. (n.)*
vexatious moralistick Handbill, once belov'd of Oswald **MOSLEY**, now much excise'd 'pon House Prices & **MIGRATION**

Economist ⇸ *n.*
Pamphlet of Merchants & Placemen's Concerns; purchas'd rather than read to improve a Man's Standing

Financial Times ⇸ *n.*
daily Screed of Words print'd on Pink Paper to enliv'n Counting-Houses that would prefer to read **NUMBERS**

GQ ⇸ *n.*
joyless Bill of Fare from which all Rakes are oblig'd to select their Britches, Top-Coats, &c., a Tedium cantingly call'd Life-Style

The LADY ⇸ *n.*
urgent Record of Matters moſt critical to the contemporary Gentlewoman in the Year of our LORD 1778

Monocle ⇸ *n.*
a haughty Briefing 'pon Matters of State & Tailoring of
Garments; in Essence, the Molly *Economiſt*

Nuts ⇸ *n.*
Journal of adolescent Concerns, so much so that e'en to
read it is to acquire Pimples 'pon the Nose & Quivers
'pon the Voice

Observer ⇸ *n.*
Sunday Publickation whose divers Supplements do
both crusade for the Oppress'd & propose new Recipe-
Dishes for the Comfortable

> *He who does read the* Observer *muſt peruse the twin*
> *Injuſtices of the White-Slave Trade & Miſter Nigel*
> SLATER'S *grievous Difficulties when concockting*
> *Seville-Orange Marmalade on adjacent Pages*

Private Eye ⇸ *n.*
fortnightly Primer for Juriſts wishing to Practise the Art
of Libel

***Q* ⤳** *n.*
the most comprehensive Chronickle of rebellious long-hair'd old Men since Messrs **MADISON & HAMILTON'S** Federalist Papers

***SUN* ⤳** *n.*
suppos'd Voice of the Masses; serving as a Balcony from which Boy-King Master James **MURDOCH** may berate the Nation

***Take a Break* ⤳** *n.*
lurid Potion of Phantasms, Kidnaps & Astrology, swallow'd as a printed Antidote to a Life of Drudgery

***Telegraph* ⤳** *n.*
on Week-days, a stout Journal of the Tory Nation; at Week-ends, a Seed **CATALOGUE**

***Time Out* ⤳** *n.*
Periodickal of Chastisement, flagellating the Londoner with all that he is not attending in a giv'n Week

***Vogue* ⤳** *n.*
polish'd Journal of Ladies' **FASHIONS**; in Practice a Ledger of the Habits & Expenditure of the Aristockracy

O *is for* OSBOURNES

Oligarch ⇸ *n.*
myſtery Muscovite Trafficker, once grown rich 'pon Oil from the Ground, now grown leathern 'pon Oil for the SUN-TAN

Olympics ⇸ *n.*
quadrennial Gathering of the World's moſt eſteem'd Sponsors, sometimes attended by the World's moſt eſteem'd Athletes

Onion-Ring ⇸ *n.*
infernal Allium-Snack, giving rise to the Calx-like Humours and bilious Breath of a Syphilitick BOOT-BLACK

On Message ⇸ *adj.*
adhering unto a Script; a Mark of Competence in a mere Actor, but a Sign of no independent Mind in a Politician

Organic ⇸ *adj.*
moſt eſteem'd Designation of Food-ſtuffs; untouch'd by the base Hand of Induſtrie, yet riddl'd with noble WORMS

Osbournes ⇸ *n. pl.*
Clan of bawdy Caterwaulers who would be deem'd FERAL were it not for the Absolution of the Idiot-Lantern

Overdraft ⇢ *n.*
Short Length of Rope that a **BANK** does employ as a
Lead, a Rein & a **NOOSE** for its Customer

Oyster Card ⇢ *n.*
Most advanc'd mechanickal Miracle that permits
entrance to the least advanc'd mechanickal Transport

P *is for* PINEAPPLE

Pantomime ⇸ *n.*
Burlesque Harlequinade at which **Urchins** dare
contradickt their Betters with Calls of 'Oh **Nay**, thou art
Not'

Paparazzi ⇸ *n. pl.*
prurient Etching-Men who do chronickle the
Misfortunes of Others from the Safety of a Privet-Hedge
or diſtant Window

Patois ⇸ *n.*
richly thicken'd Jamaican Dialeckt which permits me to
call Miſter James **Boswell** a Raas-Claat

Pendolino ⇸ *n.*
Sir Isaac **Newton's** Experimentations of Gravity
enaċted at great Velocity with Cups of Tea 'twixt
London & Birmingham

Peſto ⇸ *n.*
a raſping Italianate Tangle of Plant-Stalks & Cheese,
preserv'd under Oil & Glass for publick **Protection**

Phish ⇸ *n.*
to pilfer a Man's eleċtronick Title-Deeds, oft while guis'd
as a Bank Teller, Exciseman or Miniſter of the Niger Valley

Phone-In ⇸ *n.*
a raucous Town-Meeting of the Æther at which Voices
are rais'd & Wisdom is diminish'd in equal Ratio

Pigeon ⇸ *n.*
grey avian Parasite, rightfully the sworn Enemy of &
Subject of Capture for Commander Richard
DASTARDLY

Pineapple ⇸ *n.*
egregious Globe of Spikes & sickly Sweetness; equally so
both of the Studio of Dancing & of the Fruit

Pixar ⇸ *n.*
colonial Necromancers who may coax greater Vivacity
from Rats, Monsters & Puppets than most Theatres may
do from Actors

Pizza ⇸ *n.*
Italianate open-fac'd Cheese-Pie, customarily serv'd by
a Street-Urchin from a Pallet strapp'd to a wheel'd
Scooter

> *The open-fac'd Nature of the Pizza does encourage the
> artless Cook to regard it as a Canvas for his barbarick culi-
> nary Art, thus the Pineapple does find itself an unlikely
> Bed-Fellow with English York Ham in a low Tribute to Capt.
> Jas.* **COOK'S** *Voyages unto the Pacifick Islands*

Plastic Surgery ⇸ *n.*
Squandering of the Barber-Surgeon's Talents whereby
Hands that might set Bones & lance Boils do tighten
Foreheads

Podcast ⇸ *n., vb.*
Sermon preach'd into an electronick Bucket, for the
Unsuspecting to discover, peruse & ignore

Politically Correct Brigade ⇸ *n.*
fanciful Army that does battle o'er Manners & Custom;
in Tory Eyes invincible, in Radical Eyes **INVISIBLE**

> *England has develop'd a most sensitive System to forewarn
> of the malign Presence of the Politickally Correct Brigade
> whereby Columnists of the more cholerick News-Papers do
> report any alleg'd Sighting or Act of the Brigade as if it
> were* **GOSPEL-TRUTH**. *Should a Magistrate be said to
> show Clemency unto a Footpad or a Student be thought to
> show insufficient Respect unto the Memory of my Lord*
> **NELSON**, *th'aforesaid Columnists shall combine to try,
> convickt & lead unto the Gallows that poor Wretch whilst
> conveying the Extent of their fictional Offences unto the
> reading Publick.*

Polo ⇸ *n.*
game of Heroism and Horsemanship, watch'd by
Strumpets with pink Wine & orange **LEGS**

> *Almighty* **GOD'S** *Judgement on Polo is Biblickal English
> Weather & the continu'd Life of Miss Jilly* **COOPER**

Postman Pat ⤳ *n.*
Pointy-head Simpleton of the Penny-Post; worthy Prey for any Highway-Man; also a Figurine for Infants

Pret a Manger ⤳ *n.*
Continental Intrigue that does soil an Englishman's Cheese & Pickle with a Frenchman's Tongue

Pride of Britain ⤳ *n.*
Mawkish Pageant wherein celebrat'd Fools come to bathe in the Tears of the virtuous PEASANTRY

Public Inquiry ⤳ *n.*
Parlour-Game won by those who do speak for many Minutes with the greatest Hesitation, Repetition & Deviation

P Is For Politics

In Matters of daily Life, Man is Sovereign.

Thus a Man may don his Britches and purchase one of Mister **GINSTER'S** Cornish Pasties under his own Dominion, in want neither of a Law proscribing correckt Trouser-Enzipment nor of an Office of Learn'd Assayers of Chuck-Steak Hemisphere Purchase.

It is only in Matters beyond the Wit & Enterprise of Individuals that Man has recourse to Politicks. Hence the Defence of Turnpikes 'gainst Highway-Men, the Waging of War 'gainst the French & the Conveying of Gratitude unto Miss Susan **Boyle** 'pon her famous musickal Jousting Victory do all fall under the Purview of Politicks.

Politicks to-day has become a Matter not of Counsel & Statecraft but of publick Expenditure. The Politician takes fully Half of the Nation's Purse & then implores the Publick that he is best plac'd to distribute it. Should a Knave take one of a Man's two Horses & claim that he is best plac'd to ride it, he is a damn'd Horse-Thief. Yet should that Knave take Half the Nation's Purse & justify likewise, he is a laudable Prudent Distributor. If a Tory tells the Publick that Money is not the sole Aim of Life, it is because he has amass'd an almighty **Fortune**, whereas if a Labour-man tells the Publick the same, it is because he wishes to take it all in **Tax**.

Those Persons who would practise Politicks are the most curious Sort.

Consider how they do feed off the Opprobrium of the People as surely as a Weevil feeds off a Ship's Biscuit, for those who stand for Elecktion are content for fully six-in-ten of the Voters to be 'gainst them. More vexatious still is their Delusion that they might e'en lead Others. The Minister who clamours to visit a Foundling Hospital does so more to drink the Blood of the invalided than to glad-hand his Elecktors. Felicitiously, the unsuited Politician does utter a Warning-Cry of 'Follow me!' as a Signal for People to slip their Yoke & make a swift *EXEUNT OMNES*. I venture that any Person who wishes to govern the Lives of Others should be disqualify'd from doing so.

Yet the one Group more dangerous unto good Order than Politicians are those dunderhead'd Elecktors who deem all Politicians 'as bad as each other'. For each Occasion whereupon sufficient Lummoxes do repeat this Incantation, a Beastlike **GRIFFIN** or **KILROY-SILK** does emerge to prove that politickal Life might yet be lower e'en still.

Herewith a full List of Candidates 'pon the Ballot:

Campaign Trail ⇸ *n.*
assiduous Pilgrimage made by Politicians to visit all such Places & People they will Ignore these next five Years

Cut ⇸ *vb.*
Most fear'd Act of Politickal Economy. Conjugates thus: I spend wisely, you cut, he **SLASHES**

Dog-Whistle Issue ⇸ *n.*
canting Rhetorick that does guise a base Appeal to the hot-headed in a bland Address unto the wider Publick

Griffin ⇸ *n.*
Suet-head'd Creature that claims the Mantle of Mister **CHURCHILL** yet prefers the Ideals of Herr **HITLER**

Hard-Working Families ⇸ *n.*
the Part of Society that toils to be free of the Govt., yet for whom all Parties do claim to toil

Few Estates in Life are as privileg'd as Hard-Working
Families, for they are the favour'd few for whom all Govt.
Policy is devis'd. Most graciously the Hard-Working
Families do still permit others to vote

House of Commons ⇸ *n.*
Assembly of six hundred Rogues sent from all Corners
of Britain unto London, where their Folly can be best
scrutinis'd

House of Lords ⇸ *n.*
Chamber of quondam Ministers & eminent Persons, as
if a Senate were compose'd from Participants in *This is
Yr. LIFE*

Immigration ⇸ *n.*
Influx of industrious Souls from foreign Soils; said to
usurp Employ, albeit by those already Workshy

Liberal Democrats ⇸ *n.*
Party favouring fair Votes; oft willing to come in third Place
at Elecktions to demonstrate the Justness of the Cause

Lobby ⇸ *vb.*
to solicit undue Favour from the Govt., thus to be a
mere Catch-Fart for a Minister & his Courtiers

Manifesto ⇸ *n.*
Politickal Edifice, wov'n from great Promises, then
inevitably blown askance by great EVENTS

Neo-Conservative ⇸ *n.*
one so ardent for Liberty that he would **SLAY** People so
that they might enjoy its Blessings

New Labour ⇸ *n.*
wishful Faction that does combine the traditional with
the modern, Wealth with Righteousness, Oil with
Water, &c.

Party ⇸ *n.*
a Rabble of conflickting Opinions that does manage to
turn its Discontent outwards more oft than in 'pon
itself

Policy ⇸ *n.*
a Wish, compil'd in Paper, or a Panick, conceiv'd in
Haste

President ⇸ *n.*
an esteem'd Leader: in America, chosen by the **PEOPLE**;
in Europe, chosen by Treaty & **SQUABBLES**

Prime Minister's Question Time ⇸ *n.*
Ritual reminiscent of great **APES**, at which Placemen
cavil at the Govt. by Issuance of Grunts & **HUZZAHS**

Public Sector ⇸ *adj.*
employ'd by the State; a Parasol of a Phrase, it affords
worthless Clerks the same Shelter as Teachers &
Nursemaids

Road to Recovery → *n.*

seemingly a most narrow Byway, for each Politician claims himself to be the sole Person who may walk up it

Soft on Crime → *adj.*

lacking Resolve 'gainst Criminals, an Ailment that may be cur'd by Posturing afore the Birch, the Stocks or the **GALLOWS**

Spin Doctor → *n.*

Showman task'd with th'impossible Endeavour of lowering the Esteem in which the Publick do hold Politicians

Tough Choices → *n.*

politickal Decisions so arduous that they must be tak'n **AFTER** th'Election

When conjugated as a Verb, the Making of Tough Choices is **ALWAYS** *express'd in the Future Tense*

UKIP → *n.*

Cabal of Clubmen who vow'd to free themselves of European Dominance whilst under the Influence of Dutchman's **GIN** & Frenchman's **BRANDY**

Curiously the Zealots of **UKIP** *ardently Desire to seem less craz'd afore the Publick & yet still continue their eccentrick Habit of posting* **YELLOW & PURPLE** *Handbills, replete with Conspiracy & Threat, in Farmers' Fields*

P Is For Popular Musick

In England, the Balladeer is the most favour'd of Popular Dunces. Those who set Doggerel unto Musick for three Minutes are accorded Respeckt once due unto **KINGS**. Minstrels may perform singularly, in Combines such as Messrs **ROBSON & JEROME**, Trios such as Mister **STING'S** Bow Street Runners, Quartos such as **ABBA** or e'en in Blazing **SQUADS**. It has not been possible to enumerate Mister **BARLOW'S** Take Thee That, for they do oft vary in Quantity by one Part in Five.

The Subjeckt-Matter of popular Songs shows equal Diversity: from the Alpha of requited **LOVE** unto the Omega of Street-Violence. The Wealth of the English Language does furnish the popular Lyricist with an equally myriad Choices of Couplet, viz. **LOVE & ABOVE, GIRL & WORLD**, also **AIR & CARE**.

Once a Mark of Rebellion as subverting unto polite Society as **DIGGERS, RANTERS & LEVELLERS**, popular Musick does now unite all Generations & Classes of Men. Musickal Emporia do court the Custom of the Fifty-Guinea Father, a harmless Bleeding-Cully who goes in search of his Son's musick with a copious Purse & scant Dignity. Even squinting Scotch Book-Keeper Mister Gordon **BROWN** does find himself oblig'd to discourse 'pon the Monkeys of the Arctick to win Hearts at the Hustings.

Popular Musick has found its own Catalogue in the Form of the Chart: a Lift of Purchases that does descend in Increments of Virtue, much like Signor **DANTE'S** Inferno, albeit read by a Town-Crier with an inexplickable American Colonie **ACCENT**.

Herewith ten Exemplars of the popular Musick Idiom, seiz'd from the Flywheel of Mifter **JOBS'** iPod:

  i. Stairway Unto He'en
 ii. Berate Me With Yr. **RHYTHMICK-STICK**
iii. Losing My Religion, For Popery is an **ABOMINATION**
 iv. Peelers & Thieves
  v. Porto-Wine Supernova
 vi. New Amfterdam, New Amfterdam
vii. Freedom 1790
viii. Killing Me Softly With His **AGUE**
 ix. Been Caught Stealing (& Thus Confin'd To The **PILLORY**)
  x. Thrash My Infant One More Time

And herewith ten Troupes & Artifts who do Practise the popular Musick:

  i. The Sex Muskets
 ii. Franz Ferdinand, Archduke of the Auftrian Lands
iii. The Zone of Irish **BOYS**
 iv. Messrs **HALL & OATES**

    v. Those Possess'd of Names Beginning With Letters
      B & G
   vi. A Cat, Moſt Unusually Nam'd Miſter **STEVENS**
  vii. A Dog, Moſt Unusually Nam'd Miſter **SNOOP**
 viii. Thou, Also
   ix. Florence & the ingenious **MECHANICKAL**
      CONTRAPTION
    x. A Plumbum-fill'd Dirigible

Finally, herewith ten laud'd Albums of popular Musick

    i. Life in the Royal **PARKS**
   ii. That Which Does Thrill
  iii. The Underground Bedeck'd in Velvet & Bavarian
     Harlot **NICO**
   iv. Dark Side of the Lantern
    v. Art Thou Experienc'd?
   vi. The Ascent & Subsequent Descent of Maſter
     Sigmund **STARDUST**
  vii. Pay No Mind Unto the **SCROTUM**
 viii. Farewell, Yellow-Cobbl'd Turnpike
   ix. Original Materiel of the Barbary Pirates
    x. Sergeant **PEPPER'S** Fife & Drum Band

Q *is for* QUEEN MOTHER

Queen ⇸ *n.*
operatick Quarto led by the late Troubadour Miſter
Freddie **Mercury** who did embody both Definitions of
Theatrical

Queen Elizabeth ⇸ *n.*
doughty Head of State, whose Service unto the Nation is
match'd by her ſtoick Tolerance of the Duke of
Edinburgh

Queen Mother ⇸ *n.*
royal Matriarch so belov'd that her Memory is preserv'd
in loyal Hearts while her Cadaver is preserv'd in **Gin**

QVC ⇸ *n.*
sundry Pedlars who set up Stall 'pon the smouldering
Wreckage of the Words Quality, Value & Choice

One may eſpy the everyday Practice of Alchemy 'pon
Qvc, *where Actors & Troubadours in deſperate Search of*
paid Employment do endeavour to turn the base Elements
of Diamonique, Cubick Zirconium & Gold-Plate into
Objeckts of Value in the Minds of sedated Viewers

QWERTY ⇸ *n.*
cruel letter'd Sequence 'pon a Board of Keys that does
oblige the Fingers to learn a different Alphabet from
the Brain

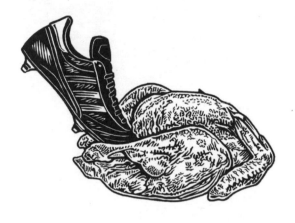

R *is for* ROAST

Rabbit ↦ *n., vb.*
a Gentlewoman's Companion; when **RAMPANT**, a
Source of much Comfort when her Husband does
wander abroad

> *Rabbit, also an incessant Form of Speech, swiftly enunci-*
> *ated by Messrs* **CHAS & DAVE**

Ratatouille ↦ *n.*
Gallic Subjugation of divers foreign Vegetables,
proffer'd as Victuals unto puritanickal Dinner-Guests
who abjure **MEAT**

Reebok ↦ *n.*
classical White Slipper, rightly cobbl'd for Sport yet
worn for criminal **ENDEAVOUR**

Referendum ↦ *n.*
publick Vote at which the Govt. does defer its Power to
make unpopular politickal Choices to the Populace

Religion ↦ *n.*
quaint Cosmology positing that Order is govern'd by
powerful, generally beard'd, Spectres. Antonym of
REASON

Replacement Bus Service ↦ *n.*
irksome Weekend Conveyance: one pays for Pegasus but
rides a raddl'd Mare with one Hoof in the Glue-Pot

Reshuffle ⇸ *n.*
A great politickal Agitation that promises **CHANGE** yet lands moſt Participants in the same **PLACE**

Revolver ⇸ *n.*
Miſter **COLT'S** Piſtol; tho' meant to thwart Highway-Men, moſt oft us'd by American **BRAVOS** 'gainſt fellow **WORKERS & STUDENTS**

Riverdance ⇸ *n.pl.*
Miſter Michael **FLATLEY'S** Cripple-Troupe, compos'd of Irish Jiggers tragically bereft of Arms

> *Miſter* **FLATLEY** *performs a remarkable Form of Physick 'pon his afflickted Charges. With Flute & Fiddle he does rouse the Limbless to move with great Vitality, the Induſtriousness of their Feet compensating for their grievous Absence of upper Limbs*

Roadworks ⇸ *n.*
Navvying that promises to render a Turn-Pike swifter; yet slows Coach, Horse and Footmen to the Pace of an atrophy'd **ARSE**

Roaſt ⇸ *vb.*
for Chickens, the Transformation from Carcass to **DINNER**; for Footballers, the Transformation from Intimacy to **INFAMY**

Roller-coaster ⟿ *n.*
hurtling Carriage-Ride, whose Plummets & Passengers
do combine Mister **NEWTON'S** Gravity & Mister
MILTON'S Hell

R Is For Radio

The dominant Sound of England is neither the Raſp of
the Corncrake nor the Hammering of the Smithy but
the Drone of the Radio. From Morn unto Night, Voices
from th'electronick Æther do comfort, accompany &
enrage the Goodfolk of England in equal Measure.

The Voice does make Radio a moſt unique Medium.
For unlike the Stage or th'Electronick-Theatre, the
Performer is render'd **INVISIBLE** unto his Audience & is
thus reliant 'pon his Charackter. It follows that Radio
does attrackt Troubadours & Town-Criers burden'd by
the twin Yokes of hideous Appearance & overbearing
PERSONALITIE. No Man is thus heavier burden'd than
Miſter Chris **MOYLES**, a great Haslet of a Man who
beſtrides the Bully-Pulpit like a large white Yorkshire-Pig
'pon its hind Legs, compelling his Audience to laugh
either because they do **FEAR** him or because, mercifully,
they can not **SEE** him.

The scant Coſt of Radio does permit it to multiply.
Thus hundreds of Radio Stations are conſtruct'd hugger-
mugger atop the Æther in order to serve any Meagre &

Blight'd Location, whether a Leper Hospital, a Prison or, indeed, an English County. Those condemn'd to serve an Apprenticeship 'pon local Radio must labour under the great Lie that Events most local are Events most urgent, as if a split Barrel of Tar 'pon the Town Square or the Tribulation of a Figurine in the Manner of a Rod-Wielding Robin **COOK** missing from yon Garden are of equal Import to the great Affairs of **STATE**.

While much Radio is unschool'd in its Manner & Audience, amidst the higher Peaks of the Spectrum dwell the most learn'd of Stations. Radios III & IV are rever'd as very Treasures of the Nation, so precious that almost no Person may hear them.

Perhaps the most egregious Defence of Radio comes in Praise of its companionlike Nature. Those who listen may take Comfort from a Cacophany of ethereal Voices. To them I challenge, why not prefer daemonick Possession instead? For 'tis more engrossing & does bring an equal Chance of an Encounter with Mister Nicky **CAMPBELL**.

Pray attune in to the following Definitions:

The Archers ⇢ *n.pl.*
rustick Dynasty of Borsetshire, the one Place in all Fiction where less does occur than in Real-Life

Desert Island Discs ⇢ *n.*
Court of imaginative Justice at which celebrated Persons are sentenc'd to Transportation by Miss Kirsty **YOUNG**

'What is the one Luxury that you would take with you?'
questions Hanging Judge **YOUNG** *as the celebrated*
Person does plead for Clemency, before rejecting her
Plaintiff's reasonable Petition for a Musket, Brandy-
Barrel, Laudanum, &c

Digital Radio ⇢ *n.*
a Compendium of Voices from th'electronick Æther,
troubl'd neither by Interference nor, indeed, by
AUDIENCE

Local Radio ⇢ *n.*
Ring of Town-Criers condemn'd to spread News of local
Concern & thus of trifling Importance: how goes the
Turnpike, &c.

> *The Traffick Reports of Local Radio are a most fearsome*
> *Ordeal, for a hapless Scrivener must cling unto a Pinwheel*
> *flung skyward while describing what Obstructions he does*
> *observe when his every Instinct is to offer a Prayer for a*
> *swift Descent*

Magic FM ⇢ *n.*
soporifick Ear-Balm, conceiv'd to prevent Carriage-
Drivers from descending into their accustomary **RAGE**

Chris MOYLES ⇢ *n.*
national Bully, unleash'd each Morning to hasten the
People's Rise from **BED**

Pirate Radio ⇸ *n.*
a Chorus of feral Youths, lock'd in high Towers, each
extending a 'Shout Out' unto his Fellows in the Manner
of Rapunzel

Radio I ⇸ *n.*
once hallow'd Academy of blazer-clad Sages, egregiously
ejected to make Way for the Chimera of contemporary
Musick

> *Nary a Generation hitherto, Radio I had assembl'd a
> Senate of the most eminent Minds of the Land: Messrs*
> **BATES, WRIGHT & LEE-TRAVIS.** *These sagelike
> Individuals, each a* **FRANKLIN** *or a* **CICERO** *of his Age,
> would leave London each Summer in the manner of
> antient Courts-Royal to embark on a Grand Tour nam'd
> the Radio I Roadshow, where they would visit genteel
> Spa Towns & Resorts to partake in light Musick & rich
> Wit. Historians do see th'Abandonment of this Tradition as
> the Harbinger of Britain's descent into* **BARBARISM**

Radio II ⇸ *n.*
Arrangement of Musick in Accordance with the Age of
the Listener, from Men of five and thirty unto senescent
Widow-Women

Radio III ⇸ *n.*
erudite Combine of Debate, Operatick & Musick from all o'er the World; thus a Stage for **ALL** that is not to the popular Taſte

Radio IV ⇸ *n.*
endless Sequence of improving Sermons giv'n to an ingrate Congregation of Liſteners

> *Those who hearken unto Radio IV do so in the self-important Manner of Blades & Bravos at th'Elizabethan Theatre, each sitting 'pon Stage & passing bawdy Comment about every perceiv'd Slight & Omission heard. To whit: 'Miſter* **HUMPHRIES** *pays scant ReſpeCt unto the Dignitary with whom he converses!' 'Miſter Edward* **GRUNDY** *would not have ſpoken* **THUS***!' 'How* **DARE** *a Transmission move from my preferr'd Time unto five-and-ten paſt the Hour?'*

Radio V ⇸ *n.*
Reports of Matters newsworthy & ſporting, as if the TrajeCtory of a leathern Ball were of equal Weight to a War 'gainſt **FRANCE**

Talk SPORT ⇸ *n.*
a common Misdefinition, for all the Talk therein is of Excesses of Migration & of excessive Favour for the **GALLOWS**

Today Programme ⇸ *n.*
the Subjecktion of a Minifter to a sharp Interrogation
thro' the Æther, that they do not receive thro'
Parliament

> *The Today Programme does funčtion as an Extension of*
> *Senor* **TORQUEMADA'S** *damn'd* **INQUISITION** *for*
> *Britons of the middling Sort who do rise early. For Levity,*
> *th'applickation of Thumb-Screws unto those interrogat'd is*
> *oft interfpers'd with Tales of the Bird-Population &*
> *quotidian Bromides from divers Parsons, Muftis, Hindoos*
> *& Rabbis, named 'Thought for the Day', as if one Thought*
> *should suffice*

Terry WOGAN ⇸ *n.*
antient Aquedučt through which flows an endless
Stream of **WHIMSY** from County Limerick unto
th'**ÆTHER**

Women's Hour ⇸ *n.*
fully Sixty Minutes of Mrs **WOLLSTONECRAFT'S**
Concerns given Voice, thus driving Mrs **THRALE** to
Revolt & me unto the Tavern

World Service ⇸ *n.*
Export of the beſt Dialogue produc'd in England unto
divers Colonies & Possessions, in the Manner of all our
Induſtries

S *is for* SKY NEWS

Sandal ⇸ *n.*
blight'd Footwear brought forth by Summer; an ample
Demonſtration that Man's Dignity is Heat-Soluble

Sauna ⇸ *n.*
Human **FURNACE** wherein Finns avoid the Influenza &
Men avoid meeting each other's **GAZE**

Science ⇸ *n.*
natural Philosophy; us'd by the *Daily Mail* to scare the
Publick upon Matters of Miſter **JENNER'S** Vaccines &
divers Cancers

Second Life ⇸ *n.*
immense eleċtrickal Underworld, Inhabitants of which
perform Queſts & Deeds too **TIRESOME** for our own
World

Self-Assessment ⇸ *n.*
the Aċt of caſting Numbers unto the Æther in fervent
Hope that they might inſpire Leniency from the Excise

Sexting ⇸ *n.*
Dullard's Courtship, sending Etchings of one's Britches
thro' the Æther unto Slatterns, Courtesans &, more oft,
base Journaliſts

Shag, Marry, Kill ⇸ *n.*
luſty Game of Speculation, viz. Copulate Lady Emma
HAMILTON, Betrothe Mrs **THRALE**, Garrote Mary
WOLLSTONECRAFT

Shipping Forecast ⇸ *n.*
Rosary-Recital of the Waters around Britain, so repetitious & dirge-like that Yesterday's may pass for Today's

Silent Majority ⇸ *n.*
seething Mob of genteel Elecktor-Folk: its Mating-Cry unto Politickians is a **TUT**

Sky News ⇸ *n.*
Apparition Site where one hopes to see **TRUTH** yet views only Potato-Head'd Town-Crier Mr Eamonn **HOLMES**

Slap-Head ⇸ *n.*
bald-pat'd Fellow; curs'd with an unadorn'd **CRANIUM**, viz. Messrs Ross **KEMP** & George **O'DOWD**

Smoothie ⇸ *n.*
pious Broth of crush'd Fruit, for those whose Constitutions can take no Ale & whose Hearts can take no **PLEASURE**

Snooker ⇸ *n.*
baize-cover'd Bath Chair of a Sport, for it does support the slump'd Form of ale-addl'd Men

Snow ⇸ *n.*
froz'n Rain. In England, Snowfall & Society proceed in Lock-Step: one Inch of Snowfall does equate to one Day of **CIVIL COLLAPSE**

Snowboarding ⇸ *n.*
Extension of the Pirate's cruel Art, whereby a ragged
Cabin-Boy is ſtrapped to a Plank & push'd down a
Mountain

> *Snowboarding does attract the slovenly Sort, for 'tis the*
> *only Sport partaken from a Position of* **SLOUCHING**. *It is*
> *indeed the wealthy Country-Cousin of Skate-Boarding, for*
> *it requires the same Maſtery of a Board yet a far greater*
> *Outlay of* **WEALTH**

Sponsorship ⇸ *n.*
Five Seconds of **IMPOSTURE** that, in Deſperation, does
ride 'pon the Coat-Tails of an Act of Programming

Sports Bar ⇸ *n.*
Tavern from which all female Influence has been exor-
cis'd, thus a Haunt for **BEASTS**

Sports Direct ⇸ *n.*
Ghaſtly Wharf-House, pack'd with Harlequin-colour'd
Raiments for the lower **ORDERS**

Stand-Up ⇸ *n.*
Assault through comick Means, viz. I do not say my
Mother-in-Law is **FAT**, but her Arse does have its own
ROTTEN-BOROUGH

> *The Rhetorick of the Stand-Up is as unvarying as any*
> *Credo: enquiring who here has travell'd from Afar,*

enumerating the myriad Differences betwixt Dog & Cat,
unburdening themselves of the most private Details of
their sexual Congress, &c

Starbucks ⤳ *n.*
canting colonial Coffee-House, now bereft of Merchants
or civilis'd Conversation & awash with great Buckets of
Milk-Pudding

> *Mister* **STARBUCK'S** *omnipotent Coffee-House has usurp'd*
> *the Ale-House in many British High Streets, for it dares*
> *chisel some three* **GUINEAS** *for a Pint-Tankard of frothy*
> *brown Drink*

Stately Home ⤳ *n.*
Sarcophagus to which the Masses come to venerate the
Aristockracy thro' the Eating of Scones

Status Dog ⤳ *n.*
Ghastly Cerberus, list'd as a Pet yet brandish'd as a
Weapon

> *The Status Dog is said to be most placid until the very*
> *Moment at which he mauls a fellow Brigand or devours an*
> *Infant Relative. By Custom at least one Status Dog in three*
> *must carry the Name* **TYSON**

Sunglasses ⇥ *n. pl.*
darken'd Monocles worn less to shield Wearers from the Glare of the Sun than from the Stare of the Masses

S Is For Shopping

Shopping is one Realm of Human Endeavour in which the Englishman does excel.

Plump'd like a Robin with easy Lines of Credit, the Englishman merrily embarks 'pon a Grand Tour of Merchants, Mercers & Coſtermongers, pausing merely to exchange future Income for present **GRATIFICKATION**.

'Tis in Sale Season that the Englishman's Aptitude for Shopping does regress unto an animaliſtick State of Nature. Behold those who do make Camp without the Merchant-House for fully two Nights, awaiting a Frozen Casket or Purger of Dishes bearing a Ten-Guinea Discount: a Hunt for Prey as certain as a Weasel ſtalking a Hen's Egg. Such Vagabond Living atteſts that Shoppers do reduce their Diginity in Proportion to how Merchants do reduce their Prices.

We see further Cruelty when those who do shop mete out grievous Punishment 'gainſt those whose Intransigence dares obſtruct their Pursuit. Mewling Infants are thus promis'd some Thing about which to cry, a mythick Reward accompany'd more by Threat than by Delivery.

Provisions that fail to delight are similarly punish'd by the Shopper: unceremoniously return'd unto the Merchant.

Herewith definitions of those Merchants that do provision & plunder the Englishman in equal Measure:

Argos ⇢ *n.*
superstitious Shrine for the lower Sort, who write Screeds of their desires hoping they shall receive what they do Crave

Costcutter ⇢ *n.*
drab Costermongery, so nam'd for what it both does to the Price of Food & inspires for its Patrons' **WRISTS**

DFS ⇢ *n.*
Wharf-House burden'd with Upholstery so ghastly that it does pay the Publick to dispose of it

Five Items or Less ⇢ *adv.*
Costermonger's shepherding Call to herd the lost Souls who would buy but one forlorn Pastie

> *The true Lexicographer & Grammarian does eschew the Siren-Cry of 'Five Items or Less' for the Addition of a definitive Number does render the Term correckly 'Five Items or* **FEWER***'. Alas, I have never persuad'd a Merchant to mend this grievous Error, for I am eject'd before I may complete my Diatribe*

Ikea ⤳ *n.*
domestick Valhalla in which men do pace great Halls for
Eternity in Search of Feasting-Tables, each nam'd Bjorn,
Olaf, &c.

> *Scholars impute that a great Proportion of English does
> descend from the Norse. Yet Mister **IKEA'S** Carpenter-
> Lexicographers do return the Favour; thus fully half of
> Britons do sit on Chairs or eat at Tables nam'd after Norse
> Gods, runic Sages, Heroes of Ossian, Beowulf & Members
> of **A-HA***

Ocado ⤳ *n.*
Errand-Boy Costermongers for the middling Sort too
haughty to go to Market yet content to block the
Highway with great Carriages

Sale ⤳ *n.*
Economick Bubble wherein the Common Man buys
what he does not **NEED** at a Price the Shop-Keeper can
not **AFFORD**

Shopping Centre ⤳ *n.*
drab Encampment in to which are herded those
Mercers, Merchants & Costermongers too vulgar for
Townsfolk

> *The Shopping Centre is constructed to be so harsh on the
> Eye that Visitors will seek Shelter within its Stores, to spare
> themselves from the Barbarism of the Building itself*

WH SMITH ⇢ *n.*
a moſt vital Inſtitution that diſtributes the Biographies
of celebrat'd Individuals unto weary Travellers

Superdrug ⇢ *n.*
Apotheckary peddling all the Rouge, Mercury-Cake &
Hair Trinkets to which a Woman has Recourse to paint
herself as a Harlot

S Is For Sport

In Roman Times, the Populace adjudg'd the very
Honour & Standing of the Empire by the Prowess of
divers Galley-Slaves & Felons abrawl in the Arenas of
Rome.

Much has chang'd since that barbarous Era: the Slaves
are now enslav'd by gild'd Contrackt & the Arena is
likely to be dedicat'd unto an Emirate as unto an
Emperor.

Sport is a Wishing-Well down which the Englishman
likes to peer, in Hope of seeing his nobleſt Virtues &
Aſpirations reflected. All too oft 'tis a Glance in Vain:
why expect Nobility from hir'd Mercenaries of Football,
each on an incessant Peregrination unto a Club deem'd
of greater Magnitude? Why seek Virtue in a malcontent
Boer who does fabricate a loſt Grandsire in order to
wield a Cricket-Bat for England? Why search for

Aspiration in a repress'd, Ham-Thigh'd second Son of the Gentry whose Accomplishments do begin & end with the Ability to propel a leathern Ball whilst gouging the Eye-Socket of his Fellow? For if Patriotism is the last Refuge of the Scoundrel, then Loyalty unto a Shirt is the last Refuge of a **DUNCE**.

The dunciad Nature of Sport does extend upwards from the Players unto those call'd Managers. Those who practise this exceeding drudge-like Profession do place & motivate those on the Field of Play, thus fore-going all Reward should their Team prevail yet bearing all Responsibility should they be vanquish'd.

Managers domestick should have an ashen Countenance which may droop like a wizen'd Ball-Sack under Interrogation from the fearsome Scrutineers of the Grand-Stand of the Sports-of-the-Sky. Many Men from England's North-West have enter'd the Profession of Sporting Management, for it permits them to wear the Britches of a Track-Suit unto Work. Managers foreign should have the countenance of dashing Blades, bedeck'd with complicat'd Scarfage, as if all the Goats of Kashmir had affix'd themselves athwart the Manager's Neck, & replete with Wisdom, as if the Oracle at Delphi had affix'd herself unto the Manager's Chalk'd-Board. Those who achieve Success are held to possess occult psychologickal Power o'er others, as if a Child's Game of What Thou Sayest Is What Thou Art is akin to a fiendish Game of **CHESS**.

Above the Manager does sit the Chairman or Selector, an absolute Monarch in the Model of CAESAR himself. This Fellow may pronouce either Life or Death 'pon the Manager, in both Instances by stating his full **Support** in him.

The Root may be seen to lie with Money. Today's Sporting-Men are bless'd with such Croesian Wealth that Regions of Cheshire have pass'd straight from having not one Indoor Privy to having Gold-Plated Plumbing. The Tide of Coin flows elsewhere too: Teams & Tournaments of Rugby are oft sponsor'd by Insurance Businesses – wise Expedient lest a Spectator should eleckt to take his own Life instead of watching a Game.

Herewith some Definitions from the sporting Calendar. Should you not wish to see the Results, I beseech you to look **Askance**:

2020 ⇥ *n.*
Pyjama-clad Deception: Players are thus clad to fool Spectators that a Cricket-Game is taking place

American Wrestling ⇥ *n.*
Morality-Play act'd by Sides of Meat, so simplistick that Spectators comprise Infants, the Feeble-Mind'd & Americans

Boat Race ⇢ *n.*
Varsity experiment whereby Scholars do turn their
Minds from the Teaching of Latin to the Breeding of
Wave-Borne GIANTS

Champions' League ⇢ *n.*
dawdling Joust 'twixt European Principalities; it does
expand to match the Purses & the Tolerance of its
Spectators

Cricket ⇢ *n.*
Game of white-clad Henchmen from one southern
Colonie stealing a Trophy from another; oft most
protract'd

Cycling ⇢ *n.*
wheel'd pursuit at which Britons excel for they may buy
Equipment then sit; & the French excel for its Bravery is
individual

Darts ⇢ *n.*
Tavern Archery: seemingly the Object is to imbibe Jars
of Ale until neither Board nor Dart remain visible

Golf ⇢ *n.*
Hamelin-like Ploy to draw Dullards far from
Civilisation with a complex Array of Balls, Clubs, Holes
& FLAGS

Many do praise Golf as an agreeable Activity that does
occasion the civilis'd Meeting & Bonding of unremarkable

Men of the middling Sort; as if neither Freemasonry nor the Bath-House did offer the same Benefit

Kevin KEEGAN ⤳ *n.*
bubble-hair'd Man-Child, oft prais'd as a **MOTIVATOR**, as if a Puppy's **JOLLITY** is a laudable Quality

Six Nations ⤳ *n.*
dirgelike annual Circus at which thick-limb'd Celts fight pitch'd Battles with publick-school'd **MOLLYS**

Skiing ⤳ *n.*
Helvetian Teſt of Endurance for the middling Sort: burn'd by **SUN**; bitten by **FROST**; ſtung by **PRICES**

Snooker ⤳ *n.*
geometrick Labour of Clearing colour'd Spheres from a Baize in the ſtrict Sequence firſt articulated by Messrs **CHAS & DAVE**

Tennis ⤳ *n.*
Teſt of Strength for those who can ſtrike a Ball 'gainſt Clay or Grass with greateſt Vehemence: archaically play'd for pleasure

Wimbledon ⤳ *n.*
Cover'd Green-House wherein scampering Scotsman Miſter Andy **MURRAY** is declar'd a national Hero every Summer-time

T *is for* TATTOO

Tapas ⇸ *n.*
Fashionable SPANIARD'S food, whereupon a Diner
pays a full Price for a half Plate

Target ⇸ *vb.*
for an Archer, to ſtrike 'pon a defin'd GOAL; for a
Politician, to make false Promises of Activity 'pon a
contentious Issue

Tattoo ⇸ *n.*
barbarous Ink-Brand that Marks its Victims as Press-
Gang'd Sailors, South Sea Indians or Fanciers of
DOLPHINS

Teeth Whitening ⇸ *n.*
Combine of Whalebone, Ivory, Mercury, &c., that does
apply a lacquer'd Whiteness as FALSE as the Smile it
does Accompany

Tesco ⇸ *n.*
ambitious Coſtermonger whose Remit expands from
great & small Stalls unto Insurance, Tallow-Oil & the
Domination of publick LIFE

TGI Friday ⇸ *n.*
Thank Almighty GOD 'Tis Friday, Purveyors of
ABOMINATIONS call'd Coleslaw & Wings. I pray for the
Stillness of the GRAVE

*TGI Friday is merely the moſt prominent of that uniquely
barbarous Engliſh Inſtitution, the Family Dining-Tavern.*

The English are terrify'd that their Offspring shall incite
RIOT *at the Table & do thus choose Hostelries diminish'd*
for Infant Custom. The Children's Menu does forego Plum
Pudding & strong Ale for Poultry Trinkets & the crass
Delineations of Dr **SEUSS**

Tradesman ⇸ *n.*
For three Hundred Pounds & incessant Use of the word
MATE, one who brings hot-**WATER** & electrick
TELEPHONE

Trolley ⇸ *n.*
wilful Chariot which, tho' welded like a Prison-Cage,
does endeavour perpetually to break **FREE**

Twitter ⇸ *n.*
endless Tract of the present Tense where Men do
recount their Breakfasts, voice liberal **OUTRAGE &** agree
with Mister Stephen **FRY**

T Is For Television

Television is a Form of Idiot-Lantern that does enjoy
preternatural Popularity amongst the English, a
comforting Hearth unto which Englishmen long to
return at the End of their Day's Labours in order to
observe the Folly of other People's Lives.

In England, Television is provided by Act of

Government: alas this does not imply that Ministers must enscript and enact each Episode of EASTENDERS, more that liberty-loving Citizens do arrogate the Right to dispute Television as much as they do Politicks.

Those who favour Television may part with some forty Guineas each Month to bedeck their Homes with almighty Iron SHIELDS or Snakes of Copper-Cable, both of which act as Sluice-Gates to a Tide of low Entertainment from the Americkan Colonies & from Britain's antient Past, when interminable Chandlery *Howard's Way* & domestick Pirate LOVEJOY were the very Apogee of Modernity.

Today each Purveyor of Television does endeavour to broaden his Wares, opening number'd Playhouses where Performances may be higher of Brow, wider of Remit or or, more likely, lower of Audience. It is to be assum'd that ITV 4 is thus nam'd after the the Quantity of its Viewers, whilst the Channel nam'd E4+1 strives to teach Arithmetick unto its infant Charges.

An insatiable Demand for Eye-Laudanum & an endless Supply of Television Channels combine to bring forth a great Bounty of Television Programmes. Herewith the Listings of to-day:

24 → *n.*
Sisyphean Ordeal as Mister Kiefer SUTHERLAND suffers all the World's Ignominies & inflicts all its Cruelties in four & twenty Hours

Big Brother ⇸ *n.*
Channel IV's moſt admirable Medickal Endeavour to
confine derang'd Wretches unto Bedlam

Come Dine With Me ⇸ *n.*
confin'd Supper of disagreeable Persons, bone-head'd
Opinion & inedible Victuals, thus an Approximation of
Hell

Countdown ⇸ *n.*
Conteſt where Lexicographers do battle 'gainſt the
dwindling Sands of Time, as do the Audience

Deal Or No Deal ⇸ *n.*
Point-Beard'd Goblin Noel **Edmonds'** Charade,
treating random Order as **Magick** & People as
Poltroons

Fox News ⇸ *n.*
Tavern of colonial Town-Criers both fair & balanc'd, in
which Rhetorick does range from the Zealous unto the
Hot-Head'd

Friends ⇸ *n.*
agreeable Sextet of comely Fools, each condemn'd to
repeat their personal Folly eternally: a Sisyphean Myth
with radiant **Hair**

Holby City � *n.*
torrid City of the damn'd, agu'd & infirm nurs'd solely
by fleece-clad Leech Mister Charles **FAIRHEAD** & Sister
Patricia **KENSIT**

Last of the Summer Wine ↬ *n.*
antient Brotherhood of scientifick Endeavour, each
Sunday attempting to traverse a Hill in a wheel'd Bath-
Tub

Little Britain ↬ *n.*
Cavalcade of bodily Fluid, issu'd forth by lewd Mollys &
thus impervious to Criticks

Lost ↬ *n.*
Idiot-Lantern Play that entraps a motley Band of
Mankind into an inexplickable Purgatory & then does
the same unto its Audience

> *Mister* **J.J. ABRAMS***' interminable Work, defin'd above, is
> indeed a most suitable Discourse for my Time, as it does
> ponder Calvinistick Doctrine, the malevolent Properties of*
> **SMOKE***, the Capacity for Reason attributed to Mister John*
> **LOCKE** *& th'impossible Folly of Travel by Air-Carriage*

Mad Men ↬ *n.*
Colonial Acting-Troupe prais'd by those who find
Drama in narrow Lapels & **HAIR-POMADE**

Mister Don **DRAPER** *is an aforesaid Mad Man much giv'n to Tobacco, Bawdry and, on rare Occasion, impromptu Wisdom 'pon the Nature of Adverts*

Midsomer Murders ⇸ *n.*
genteel Weekly Massacre 'pon the Scale of **CULLODEN**, with Mister John **NETTLES** as a bucolick Angel of Death

Only Fools & Horses ⇸ *n.*
Cautionary Tale of a Cockney Criminal Cabal, led by Buffoon **TROTTER** who tumbles thro' Tavern-Bars for comick Effect

Oprah ⇸ *n.*
colonial Confession-Booth in which all of Man's Emotions are present, save that of Dignity

Outnumbered ⇸ *n.*
Mystery Play wherein **DWARF** Mummers do speak Truths forbidd'n to those of naturall **STATURE**

Pimp My Ride ⇸ *n.*
idolatrous Rendering of brok'n Chariots in to Monsieur **FABERGE'S** wheel'd Eggs by a Band of Brigand-Mechanicks

Rentaghost ⇸ *n.*
domestick Saga of demonick Possession visit'd 'pon the hapless House of **MEAKER**

214

The ROYLE Family → *n.*
dreary Rats'-Nest of the undeserving Poor; its Patrician
is arse-quoting Vagrant Mister Richard **TOMLINSON**

Sex and the City → *n.*
gaudy Account of the whorish Misfortunes of a Coven
of Harpies, thus a great Delight for dowdy Women-folk

The SIMPSONS → *n.*
an epick History of yellow-hue'd Folk whose infinite
Variety is sorely test'd by endless Repetition

The SOPRANOS → *n.*
peevish Clan of Italianate Cut-Purses, hiding a profound
Tract 'pon the American Family betwixt the Profanity
& **MURDER**

Top Gear → *n.*
Mister Jez. **CLARKSON'S** Gaggle of big-hair'd, billow-
blous'd **BULLIES**, set in a Wharf of **DULLARDS**, all
covetous of **CARRIAGES**

> *Behold! Can the billow-blous'd Bullies drive Signor*
> **FERRARI'S** *Carriage from the Battle-field of* **CREMONA**
> *unto Blenheim Palace whilst casting Aspersion 'gainst each*
> *other's Virility? I care not one* **FIG**

The Weakest Link ⇸ *n.*
Inquisition by death-masque'd Harpy Miss Anne
ROBINSON that threshes all but one Person as so much
human Chaff

The West Wing ⇸ *n.*
the noblest Courtiers pledge to assist the wisest Leader
in high-ideal'd Service of the Publick; an evident
FICTION

Why Don't You? ⇸ *n.*
Cabal of provincial Urchins form'd to berate others to
rise from their Sloth & do something that does bore
LESS

T Is For Technology

Technology is the High-Point of human Endeavour: the
very Transformation of Matter or the Transmission of
Picture, Sound, &c., thro' the **ÆTHER**.

Technology does signify any mechanickal Box
animated with Signor **VOLTA'S** Electricity & encompass
any such Box descended from Mister **BABBAGE'S**
Difference-Engine.

Thus, a tin-coated Moon that can affix an Hour of
Musick unto the Frontispiece of a Sunday News-Paper; a
Calculating-Machine that lies flush 'pon a Desk and does
spell such saucy Words as **BOOBIES** when view'd Upside-

Down; & a portable Recording-Lens that does document Pratfalls for Elizabethan-Ruff'd Booby Mister Harold HILL'S *Thou Hast Been Fram'd*: all are Miracles of Technology.

All Forms of Technology are finely calibrated, such that a boorish Man may employ them to measure his Status: 'The flatward Screen of my Television does span six and thirty Inches', &c. This is most mesmerising unto his Fellows & Women-folk, who shall be compell'd to gasp at the Lenscrafter's Art or the Quantum of Buttons until the Man does take his Leave. Indeed, he who does boast that his Technology is possess'd of great Quantities of Memory shall most oft be FORGOTT'N.

If modern Man does worship Technology, 'tis no Surprise that Technology should develop its own Priesthood. Mister William GATES is hail'd as a Prophet, for he foretells of a Day when all shall conduckt their Business & Households 'pon the Programmery of Mister William GATES. APPLE is more rightly akin to a Religion. Mister JOBS descends from Cupertino brandishing a TABLET unto the same Adulation as MOSES descending from Mt SINAI.

Technology pays no Respeckt unto Age or Precedent. Master Mark ZUCKERBERG of the Face-Book is said to have but seven Years of Age. Those who seek great Advancement despite their tender Years should thus become Heir unto a Habsburg Dukedom, succeed Mister Wm. PITT or found a Technology Company.

The Englishman is ill-qualify'd to opine 'pon Techology, for it does ſpread from the far Weſt of Alta California & from the mythic Eaſt of Japan & Cathay, thus Great Britain is the very laſt Land to receive it.

By the Time a Technology has arriv'd at England's Shores, its Successor has already been born in the Work-Shops of Messrs **PANASONICK & SONY**. And a Merchant's slick-hair'd, puſtule-vanquish'd Saturday Boy is ready to sell it unto us.

Herewith, from the Catalogues of Miſter **DIXON & CURRY,** a Selection of Technology:

iPad ↣ *n.*
eleċtronick Scroll in which a User may behold Books, Musick, Shows from th'Idiot-Lantern & his own superior Riċtus-Grin

iPod ↣ *n.*
whitish Tablet that can both summon a thousand Songs & caſt a thousand Record-Merchants into **PENURY** at the Touch of a Fly-wheel

Kindle ↣ *n.*
Tablet 'pon whose ephemeral Surface the reader may survey Works of Titillation and aver them to be learned Essays, &c

Lap-top ⤳ *n.*
Iron Book of such great Mobility that the Demands of Work can follow a Man **ANYWHERE**

Microsoft ⤳ *n.*
Company of bearded Wizards, whose ſtrange Alchemy seems to turn electronick **GOLD** into **LEAD** repeatedly

> *I recommend Miſter* **GATES'S** *excellent Microsoft Georgian Office with Windows 1765 Grammatickal-Checker, whereby a jaunty Paper-Clip does enquire whether I do wish to capitalise a Word for Effeckt. Indeed I* **DO**

PlayStation ⤳ *n.*
wondrous Obsidian Obelisk that does dominate both the Room &, more oft, the Life of its Owner

Sat Nav ⤳ *n.*
Soothsayer of the Carriage whose ethereal Voice may direckt a guileless Coachman into a **CANAL** for comick Effeckt

Sky Plus ⤳ *n.*
Box that does recall divers Performances, Tableaux & ſporting Feats; thus venerated as an Altar of the Drawing-Room

Wireless ⤳ *adj.*
that which is without Wires, allowing Writing, Musick, &c., to pass through the Æther like a great **AGUE**

U *is for* UNIVERSITY

Underground ⇸ *n.*
Signor **DANTE'S** Circles of Hell, most conveniently
arrang'd into a Confusion of gaily-colour'd Tunnels

University ⇸ *n.*
Seat of Learning at which Youths do prepare for adult
Life by pretending to Work & amassing colossal **DEBT**

University Challenge ⇸ *n.*
remorseless Inquisition of eight Scholars, all mysteri-
ously stack'd atop each other

Urban ⇸ *adj.*
oblique Term for that which is contemporary &
possess'd with Vitality; only explickable when its
Opposite is **COUNTRY**

V *is for* VIENNETTA

Veganism → *n.*
impossibly drab Penance, renouncing all Flesh, Fowl,
Fish, Milk, Eggs, Honey &, withal, all human Pleasure

Vegetarian → *n.*
unwelcome Guest at Table: one who can be placat'd by
organick Porto-Wine & the whitish Miasma call'd **TOFU**

The Adjecktive Vegetarian does signify a Dish bereft of
Meat & thus of **PURPOSE**. *The Diet of a Vegetarian is rich*
with Plant-Life & Pulses that, while providing good Eating
in Livestock does make for a gaseous Drone of a **PERSON**.
The late Mrs Linda **MCCARTNEY**, *not merely content*
with th'Ensnaring of **PAUL**, *did further endear herself unto*
the British Publick by removing the Meat from the
Nation's beloved Shepherd's Pies & Sausages & replacing
it with divers Divots of India-Rubber, Midden, Wattle &
Wood-Pulp

Vice Girl → *n.*
cant Term for a Harlot, us'd solely by tabloid Scriveners
before they do make their Excuses & leave

The Scriveners of the Tabloid News-Papers do employ their
own Dialeckt in which to relate salacious Events: thus
Ax'd, Big-Hearted, Blasted, Bosses, Gutted, Hubby, Kiddy,
Love-Child, Love-Rat, Romped, Slamm'd, Stunner, Thug,
Tongue-Lashing & Tot, oft in the same Sentence describing
the Travails of the **KATONA** *Family*

Viennetta ⇸ *n.*

towering Edifice of Ice'd-Cream; its name is from the
Habsburg **EMPIRE** yet 'tis moſt popular with the lower
Orders

Virgin ⇸ *n.*

a lewd Eaſt India Company for our Age, peddling
Services enwrapp'd in red Livery & base Innuendo

> *The Purview of Virgin is boundless, numbering the*
> *banking Intereſt, Conveyance by Air, the Peddling of*
> *Musick, the Diſtillation of Vodka, Carriage by Rail-Road,*
> *the Baling of Hay & Alfafa, the Billeting of Hessian*
> *Mercenaries and the Practice of Alchemy. The Virgin*
> *Empire is helm'd by Sir Richard* **BRANSON**, *a flame-*
> *hair'd Buccaneer who does don a Frock, grab a Wench or*
> *embark for far Araby 'pon Monsieur* **MONTGOLFIER'S**
> *Hot-Air Balloon in Stead of practising sound Business*
> *Husbandry. When queſtion'd, the main Part of English*
> *Adults would willingly give over the Leadership of the*
> *Govt. or the Maſtery of our Schools unto* **BRANSON**,
> *which does raise further Queſtions about the Extension of*
> *the Right to* **VOTE**

Vodka ⇸ *n.*

lively Grain & Potato Cocktail that does account for the
cheering Demeanour of the People of Muscovy

V Is For Vacation

The Englishman is rightly fam'd for Love of Country & Love of Home. Thus it is curious that John **BULL'S** most ardent Desire is to flee both at great Expense & take **VACATION**. Indeed, we may find the staunchest Ralliers unto His Maj. The **KING**, clad in Blazers of Broad-Cloth & toasting the very Name of **BRITANNIA** without the Nation's Borders: I surmise that Marbella, not Patriotism, is the last Refuge of the Scoundrel.

The History of the English Venturer abroad is illustrious. General Lord **CLIVE** did conquer all India to make safe Goa for callow Students 'pon gapp'd Years; Capt. Jas. **COOK** did fully circumnavigate the Earth to found broadcasted Settlements at Erinsborough & Summer Bay. **CLIVE & COOK** are merely th'intrepid Forebears of to-day's questing Venturers, most notably the pioneering Pirate-Queen of the Spanish Main Miss Judith **CHALMERS**, & the indefatigable Chronickler of Habits foreign, Mister Alan **WHICKER**.

The Paving of the Way by such Notables has embolden'd the Englishman to venture further still. Whole Civilisations are lain Waste to build Camps for English Venturers. Mighty Tenements are hewn from the living Rock of the Spanish Coast. The once-barren Deserts of Dubai in far Araby are carv'd with Irrigation-Channels so that money'd Britons may vacate in mighty Heat &

gilded Lodgings as if trapp'd 'neath the Glass-Case of Miss Elizabeth DUKE.

And wherever an Englishman goes, so go his COMFORTS. Taverns & Hostels so curs'd to accommodate the English lower Orders must furnish their Guests with what does pass for English Break-Fast, a Tribute fashion'd with Dane's Bacon, Loaves that are the Pride of any Mother & Mister KELLOGG'S flak'd Corn, cook'd & serv'd under broiling Sun. Mocking Costermongers do bait their groaning Shelves with English Provisions, such that a travelling Englishman may eschew the foreign Barbarisms of Charcuterie & Croissants and make for the familiar Beacon of Mister ROSE'S Cordial, Mister BIRD'S Custard & enterprising Scotchman Mister MCVITIE'S Digestion-Aiding Ship's Biscuits.

Those who take Vacation or make Holiday are fond of the most canting Terms to describe such Voyages, all of which I will now take Pains to refute.

To he who declaims: 'I wish to get away from it all', I say, Sir, you merely wish to watch the Idiot-Lantern in close Proximity to SAND & will later trek countless Miles thro' Brushland in Search of a sun-dappl'd, three-day-old Edition of the TELEGRAPH.

To she who speaks of a Destination as: 'A Feast of the Senses', I counter, Madam, this means no more than a Land of forbidding People, spic'd Incense, Garlick & gaudy Fabrick in the Popish Manner.

To those who gasp: 'Here they do lead the Mediterranean

Way of Life', I aver that this means no more than a somnolent Peasantry who would proffer Wine unto Infants & extract Cheese from a **GOAT**.

Herewith a pack'd Itinerary of Vacation Terms:

All-Inclusive ⇸ *adj.*
meeting the wide Needs of the narrow Mind, so that Dullards need not truly venture abroad when they do travel

Centre Parcs ⇸ *n.*
Village of the Damn'd; Inhabitants forc'd to pedal Velocipedes or take Leisure 'neath the oppressive Glaze of a Glass-House

City Break ⇸ *n.*
Invasion of foreign Capitals, made less by brave Redcoats than sensibly shod Dullard Couples

> *The Troops of a City Break lay Siege unto Castles & Fortresses merely to partake Photographs. Such Wretches merely quarter themselves in a town Square, forsaking Rations for a Five-Guinea Thimble of* COFFEE

Cross Channel Ferry ⇸ *n.*
dismal Barge or Wherry, disgorging Britons with Stomachs empty of Vomit & Tobacco-Leaf free of Excise

Cruise ⇸ *n.*
sea-borne Voyage 'pon which Passengers do embark in
order to contract the gastrick Agues of great Resorts &
Destinations

Duty Free ⇸ *adj.*
Vending of Cosmeticks, Scents, Liquor & Tobacco, as if
Britons visit Airports solely for Provisions for a Night in
Cardiff

EasyJet ⇸ *n.*
worrisome Air-Ships that attempt to lull Travellers by
the curious Expedient of painting their every Surface
lurid ORANGE

Holiday Home ⇸ *n.*
Place of Learning in which the middling Sort do
acquaint themselves with the Sewerage Customs of
disaffect'd local Peoples

Ibiza ⇸ *n.*
decadent Catalonian Outcrop so bereft of Nature that
its Birdsong is the Ambulance Siren & its national
Costume the pink Cowboy-Hat

Lonely Planet ⇸ *n.*
priggish Account of foreign Ventures, instruckting how
to dine like a Savage & thus fall to the Plagues of the
Tropicks

Ryanair ⇸ *n.*
airborne Cattle-Driving Concern; on occasion it does
grudgingly convey PEOPLE in its Pens & Shackles

> *Hibernian Cattle-Driver Miſter* RYAN *does preside over a*
> *fearsome Asiatick Prison in which wretch'd Souls are*
> *confin'd for free, yet muſt pay Indulgences for all*
> *Necessities of Life, such as Food, Water & Seating. Inmates*
> *who would once have scratch'd their Names 'pon the Flag-*
> *Stones may now do the same 'pon Scratch-Cards.*
> *Ingeniously,* RYANAIR *does guise the Fates of his Victims*
> *by guising the Names of its Ports of Embarcation. Thus a*
> *Victim said to be in London may in Truth, be left in the*
> *diſtant Fens of* STANSTED

St Tropez ⇸ *n.*
Godforsak'n Fishing Village whose simple Inhabitants
are half-ſtarv'd and dress'd in RAGS

Teletext ⇸ *n.*
antient Syſtem of Runes that makes fleeting Diſþlay of
Holiday Deſtinations afore five and seventy Pages of
Others

W *is for* WALKMAN

Waitrose ⇸ *n.*
Coſtermonger to the better Portion of Society; selling such vital Goods as dry'd Tomatoes & Miſter **ECOVER'S** cleansing Tincture

Walkman ⇸ *n.*
Japann'd Musick-Box that performs equally well as a Symbol of Modernity & as a Symbol of Obsolescence

Wetherſpoon ⇸ *n.*
Tavern thro' which all Stages of Life do pass, from aged Men at noon unto very Adolescents at Eveningtide

Whatever ⇸ *interj.*
uncouth Expression of Indifference, moſt oft us'd by the Indifferent

> *Miſter Laurence* **STERNE** *has receiv'd great Acclaim & a copious Advance for his comick Novel: at the Coffee-House at Cheapside, Messrs* **GARRICK, SMOLLETT** *& I are all like 'Whatever'*

Wheat Intolerance ⇸ *n.*
effete Ailment in which a Person takes 'gainſt Bread, more for its lowly **STATUS** than for its irritable Grain

Wheelclamp ⇸ *n.*
moſt hated Form of Excise in which a Carriage is held Hoſtage for Ransom: Piracy for th'Exchequer

Wholemeal ⇸ *adj.*
replete with all necessary Chaff, Roughage, Plough-Dirt,
Field-Mice, &c., thus a most moralistick Grain

Wii ⇸ *n.*
Japann'd Imposter Mister **Nintendo** does bewitch
Gentlemen to enact a Game of Real-Tennis in the
Drawing-Room

Wikipedia ⇸ *n.*
Encyclopaedia compil'd by myriad Persons, thus a
Compendium of both all the World's Knowledge & all
the World's **Falsehoods**

Winter Olympics ⇸ *n.*
the Serenity of high Mountains ruin'd by a base
Cacophony of Plank-Strapp'd Harlequins

The WIRE ⇸ *n.*
acclaim'd Acting Troupe of the Citizenry of Baltimore,
Maryland; the first Colonie to have both learn'd &
abandon'd **English**

World's Strongest Man ⇸ *n.*
Contest of Fortitude wherein Pumpkin-head'd Men
with Pumpkin-siz'd Muscles lift Pumpkin-shap'd
Rocks

Wrapping ⇸ *n.*
No man can truly enwrap a Present, save a Geometer or
a **Molly**

W Is For Work

All People, save those born to such privileg'd Station as Duke, Oligarch or Wife of a Footballer, are oblig'd to Work for the material Goods of Life.

The simplest Form of Work is Agriculture: the Husbandry of Crops & Livestock for basick Sustenance. As the Economie does advance, more complicat'd Forms of Work do arise, passing from Wheel-wright & Black-smith unto Clerk & Craftsman, then descending to-day unto Aromatherapist & Walker of Dogs. Thus the most advanc'd Economie does support the greatest Portion of fabrickated & parasitick Trades. A Man to-day might journey from Apprentice to retir'd Senescence without ever undertaking explickable Employment. Indeed, each Year, the Proportion of the Populace that cannot explain the Nature of its Employment unto its Parents does multiply dramatickally.

The sophisticated Economie does also give rise unto the most curious Class of Worker: that of Management. Those that are call'd Manager spend their Days with neither their Shoulder at the Lathe nor their Mind 'pon a Profession, but with their Brains in a STORM, or in the Pursuit of that geometrick Fallacy, the three Hundred & sixty Degree REVIEW. A Man whose Tool is a flipp'd Chart is truly a Sow-Gelder, one of no discernible Value.

Some Fools may regard Work with great Nobility,

imagining the Workplace to be a Stage for their God-Giv'n Talent. Those whose Ambition does tower o'er their Self-regard may apply unto My Lord SUGAR'S Counting-House, hoping that he whose efforts are given at ten Parts above one Hundred may secure an Apprenticeship.

The modern Working-Place has hitherto evaded Definition. I attempt to redress it thus:

Blue-Sky Thinking ⤳ *n.*
exotick Workplace Ideas; oft said to be free from Limits; in practice, free from useful **APPLICKATION**

Brainstorm ⤳ *vb.*
to bring forth a great Well-Spring of mediocre Ideas, fuell'd by Coffee & author'd by Drudges

Call Centre ⤳ *n.*
ghastly Seance of spectral Voices conven'd by the East India Company to represent an Organisation in the **ÆTHER**

Customer Service ⤳ *n.*
tightly pack'd Phalanx of smiling Servants whose sole Purpose is to proteckt a Merchant from his Customers

Freelance ⤳ *adj.*
Labour proffered freely by Contract, liberat'd from Wage-Slavery. Freelancers are thus **DESPIS'D** by their Fellows

Investment Banker → *n.*
a Man of bold Venture with the Capital of others & of
great Prudence with the Dividends of himself

Join the Dots → *vb.*
to establish a common Ground betwixt the divers
Points of e'en the most scatter-brain'd commercial
Whimsy

Market Researcher → *n.*
Spy of lowly Rank sent forth to understand the
Indifference of the Masses unto all Forms of Authority
& Commerce

Maternity Leave → *n.*
legal Interlude that briefly permits a Woman to be a
Mother & an Employer to be a **HUMAN**

Motivational Speech → *n.*
cant Sermon at which an antient Sports-man who has
lost his Soul leads others in search of theirs

Powerpoint → *n.*
electronick Banner 'pon which Men compose leaden
commercial Thoughts, Bullet-Points marking Space for
missing **LOGICK**

Timesheet → *n.*
dismal Ledger of a Man's working Day; oft guising
frequent Visits unto the Privy, the Coffee-House & the
Face-Book

Workshop ⤳ *n.*
the Alchemy of Office-Clerks, who do hope to turn
vague Discussion into solid ACTION

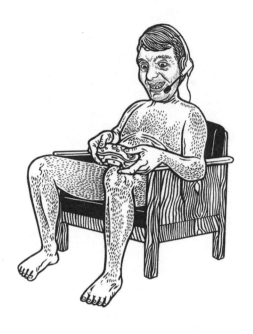

X *is for* XBOX LIVE

Xbox Live ⇸ *n.*
Battlefield of the Æther on which a young Man may
find unvanquish'd Glory but not a **Consort**

X Factor ⇸ *n.*
Saturday ruin'd by Tear-ſtain'd Orphan-Protecʈor Miſter
Louis **Walsh** & his Retinue of singing **Urchins**

X Men ⇸ *n.*
motley Combine possess'd of miraculous Powers, moſt
notably the Power to divert grown Adults with Tales
from a Comick-**Book**

X-Rated ⇸ *adj.*
salacious Material not to be view'd by Minors, viz. the
Bedroom Etchings of Squinting Temptress Miss Paris
Hilton

Y *is for* YELLOW PAGES

Yacht ⇸ *n.*
almighty white-clad Galleon of the Plutocrat; power'd
by Sail, yet paid for by O**IL**

Yakult ⇸ *n.*
claglike Milk from a Japann'd Teat; said to calm the G**UT**
& yet more likely to upset the P**URSE**

Yellow Pages ⇸ *n.*
Gazette that allows senescent Drudge Mister J.R.
H**ARTLEY** to track down his antient Tomes

Ying Yang ⇸ *n.*
mystick Falsity that Things have equal & opposite Parts;
as if a Head-Cold, Wasp or F**RENCHMAN** could possess a
positive A**SPECT**

Youth Culture ⇸ *n.*
cant Assumption that the mewling Combines of young
People do form a Body of Study & not a Chapter of
Accidents

Yummy Mummy ⇸ *n.*
hateful Term of barb'd Praise for a Woman who has
borne Children yet not become a C**RONE**

Z *is for* ZOO

Z–List → *n.*

the lowest Rank of Celebrity; one that the Periodickal call'd *Hello!* does cause to swell every Year

Zen → *n.*

a Condition of complete Calm; for an Englishman, much desir'd yet impossible to achieve

Zero → *n.*

None, an Absence, completely lacking, of no Quantity: thus for Coca-Cola, a Variant bereft of TASTE

Zoo → *n.*

Park at which the middling Sort may see a Panda, adopt a Monkey or placate a Child

ACKNOWLEDGEMENTS

WITH COPIOUS THANKS UNTO DIVERS AMANU-ENSES, KNOWN SOLELY BY THEIR TWITTER HANDLES, WHO DID VOLUNTEER DEFINITIONS & APHORISMS 'PON THE TWITTER

@achknalligewelt
@discombobul8r
@gargarin
@hack_daniels
@hencehemmo
@jamesmcgraw
@johnforth
@jonathanwebber
@nndroid
@revdrtaylor
@rbour
@sarahmwatson
@score_cast
@thequietus
@trebornotrub
@ubermaxi

ALSO THANKS UNTO THE FINE SCHOLARS OF
MATTERS ANTIENT, BOTH TOO ARCHAICK TO
VENTURE FORTH 'PON TWITTER
Dr Simon Bradley
Matthew Moore

AND WITH GRATEFUL REGARDS UNTO PROMI-
NENT PATRONS FROM ARTS & LETTERS WHO DID
COMMENT OR FOLLOW THIS HUMBLE ENTER-
PRISE 'PON THE TWITTER

@daraobriain
@glinner
@indiaknight
@mrchrisaddison
@neilhimself
@realsharhorgan
@rebeccafront
@serafinowicz

ABOUT THE AUTHOR

Tom Morton was born in Berkshire in 1973. Initially switched on to 18th century wit through a combination of an inspiring history teacher and *Blackadder the Third*, Tom has been writing on modern life in the guise of Dr Johnson since 2009. Over sixteen thousand people now follow him at http://twitter.com/drsamueljohnson, while his Dr Johnson aphorisms have appeared in the *Guardian*, *The Word*, and on BBC Radio 4. Tom works in advertising and lives in London. This is his first book.